TOSS YOUR OWN SALAD

Eddie McNamara

TOSS YOUR OWN SALAD

THE MEATLESS COOKBOOK WITH BURGERS, BOLOGNESE, AND BALLS

FOOD PHOTOGRAPHY BY APRIL RANKIN

ILLUSTRATIONS BY JOSH LORD
LETTERING BY JONAH ELLIS

ST. MARTIN'S GRIFFIN
NEW YORK

www.stmartins.com

Illustrations by Josh Lord
Lettering by Jonah Ellis
Designed by Steven Seighman

The Library of Congress Cataloging-in-Publication Data is available upon request.

ISBN 978-1-250-09920-4 (trade paperback)
ISBN 978-1-250-09921-1 (e-book)

Our books may be purchased in bulk for promotional, educational, or business use. Please contact your local bookseller or the Macmillan Corporate and Premium Sales Department at 1-800-221-7945, extension 5442, or by e-mail at MacmillanSpecialMarkets@macmillan.com.

First Edition: June 2017

10 9 8 7 6 5 4 3 2 1

For Meirav: my love, my partner, my muse, my everything

CONTENTS

THIS IS NOT A TYPICAL VEGETARIAN COOKBOOK

I need to say a few things up front. First, I'm not going to make you read through long-winded, bullshit prose about how the sun bounced off the fiddlehead ferns that swayed in the summer breeze in those oh-so-beautiful childhood summers in my grandmother's garden. Seriously, what the fuck is up with these twee descriptions of greenmarket produce? The rambling, hazy memories of the way desserts smelled coming out of a hot oven at a fantastic little bakery in the South of France? C'mon, people, I'm trying to make dinner over here.

Second, I'm not a sexy Italian TV personality or food trend "influencer." A lot of cookbooks are written by celebrity chefs who spend most of their time dazzling the press and taking fan selfies, or by executive chefs who lead a brigade of cooks in a commercial kitchen. Are these the people you want recipes from? What does any of that have to do with you, some schmuck at home

staring into the refrigerator and wondering what the hell you're going to eat tonight? Nothing, that's what. I don't have a cooking show and I don't work in a restaurant anymore, so what I do every night in my kitchen is more relevant to what you, the home cook, are trying to do. **MAKE SOME GODDAMN DINNER.**

I'm just a regular guy from Brooklyn. (Though I live in Manhattan now. Look, ma, I made it.) I used to be a cop with the Port Authority of New York and New Jersey. On 9/11/01, I responded to the World Trade Center at 10 a.m., and worked on-site with the Rescue/Recovery team for the next nine months. I didn't know it then, but there wouldn't be any rescues. That meant my job—every day, twelve hours a day—was making recoveries. We called the smoking, unstable pile of rubble we dug through "The Pit," where we found what was left of the people we lost. Take a moment and imagine that version of reality, night after night. It marked me in ways I never even considered. It wasn't long—about five years—until I was forced to come to terms with my PTSD and panic disorder and retire my badge. My condition made me afraid to leave the apartment. During my time as an urban hermit, I figured if I was pent up at home all day I might as well make dinners for me and my wife, Meirav. I became obsessed with cooking and watched the Food Network incessantly. In a ploy to get me out of the house, she signed me up for three basic cooking classes at the Natural Gourmet Institute. And I liked them so much that I enrolled in the chef's training program.

I loved culinary school. I had enthusiastic instructors, passionate classmates, and a Xanax prescription to curb my breakout panic, just in case. My Act Two was somehow going to involve cooking. After graduation, I interned for Amanda Cohen at Dirt Candy, a then-tiny, boundary-pushing vegetable restaurant in the East Village. (Now, it's a much bigger, award-winning restaurant on the Lower East Side.) Working for my favorite chef at the best vegetarian restaurant in the world was awesome, but I wasn't about that restaurant life. I did some private chef jobs until I landed a gig doing recipe testing and development for *InStyle* magazine. Similar gigs came in from *HGTV* and *Women's Health*. It was the perfect job for someone with severe panic attacks—I did all the work from my own kitchen.

Like you, I want to eat "healthy-ish," save a few bucks, and enjoy my meals. In fact, my book is less about delighting an audience and more about documenting the food I actually make for myself and my wife every day. I don't want to eat to balance my chi or read a literary essay about a ripe eggplant. I'm honestly confused about how vegetables have been fetishized by food writers. They're vegetables. They're for putting in your mouth. And sometimes they need a little help—the right tools, spices, and techniques—to make things more exciting. This I can help you with.

Third, I don't have a weird agenda. I'm not trying to sell you branded vitamins or convince you to join a vegan militia. (By the way, let's not get all hung up on the whole vegetarian versus vegan thing. That drives me nuts.) I happen to eat a vegetable-focused diet. Most of the time. More accurately, I'm as loyal to vegetarianism as a French Prime Minister is to his spouse. Most of the time I'm good, but when something tempting falls into your lap . . . what can you do? You can count on this, though: There are no recipes in this book for boeuf bourguignon or fried chicken. All these recipes are meatless because that's how I eat at home. If I'm out to eat, it might be a whole different story.

And let's not start hating the carnivores just because they're out there eating Bambi. Vegetarian recipes are what meat-eaters ask me about the most. Either they're trying to reduce their meat consumption for a variety of reasons, or they want to eat more vegetables but aren't sure how to make them more palatable. Look, if you can't live without putting meat in your mouth, make it on the side—that's what vegetarians have to deal with their whole lives. I don't care if you're vegan, vegetarian, or your guru has requested that you eat only raw, sprouted foods. Want to live like a CrossFit caveman? Go ahead. I'm not about gimmicks or unsubstantiated health claims, and I'm not going to try to scare you or guilt you into giving up meat. My intention is to share some of my favorite recipes that are cheap, healthy, hopefully clever, and most importantly, taste awesome.

Here's the final thing I have to say: You don't need the patience of a saint or advanced knife skills or a diploma to be a great cook. Becoming a great cook takes two things: a little knowledge and a lot of practice. You don't have to go to culinary school just to make dinner. You also don't have to spend your whole paycheck at a farmers' market to cook the recipes in this book. If a recipe is simple enough for me to whip up at home, you can do it, too. It'll be tasty and (relatively) healthy, and it won't take up your whole night. Just flip to the page of the dish you want to make, grab your ingredients, and go for it. I've got your back.

When I was testing, rewriting, and developing recipes for magazines, it was my job to make sure that the recipes turned in by the chef who screamed at people on TV, or the one with the clever catchphrase or the really pretty blonde who always seemed to be in soft focus, actually looked and tasted the way they were supposed to. I spent about half the time scaling down restaurant recipes, simplifying them for a home cook, or telling my editor that the recipe was perfect just the way it was because it was amazing and some chefs are famous for good reason. The other half of the time I was breaking my ass to fix a recipe that was clearly some bullshit made up on the fly in a phone call with the publicist. If I'm paying for a cookbook, I want to be sure that the recipes are going to work. If you want Penne Tikka Masala, you can Google a random recipe and take a chance, or you can flip to page 114 and make mine, knowing that it's going to be delicious. I made it for dinner and took OCD notes. My friends have eaten it and bugged out. My editor and publisher made these recipes and loved them, too. How else do you think I got to write this book?

So, you can go to culinary school, pay about $30,000 a year, and spend a wad of cash at the greenmarket or I can tell you what I learned in the classroom and my kitchen. Let me give you a ton of awesome recipes that will blow you away and save you thirty grand in the process. Let me show you how to have a vegetarian kitchen that has burgers, Bolognese, and balls, but none of the gauzy fiddleheads. (OK, there are a few fiddleheads on page 145. So sue me.) You good with this? Let's get started.

LESSON 1
LEARN SOME BASIC KNIFE SKILLS

You don't need a fancy-ass, expensive set of hand-forged Japanese knives. You just need one decent chef's knife and a sharpener. I use the same basic Mercer chef's knife I've had since culinary school, and as long as I keep it sharp and clean it's all I'll ever need.

Now that you have a nice, sharp knife, go out and procure a big bag of onions, a big bag of celery, and a big bag of carrots. Head over to YouTube and search for a basic knife skills tutorial. (Try typing in your favorite chef's name—chances are they already have a video posted.) Watch and learn.

Watch the video a second time, this time with your knife. Start chopping, dicing, "matchsticking," "brunoising," slicing, julienning, and all that other shit you're rarely—if ever—going to need as a home cook. Don't stop until you've chopped all the onions, carrots, and celery.

LESSON 2
LEARN TO BE HANDS-ON

The best way to become a better home cook is to be hands-on. I'll be your cooking instructor—just do what's written on the page. Read the whole thing first. (Don't skim it, read it.) Then do it. Once you've got a dish down, maybe you can improve on it. Go ahead and change it up. Substitute out ingredients or add new ones, with a focus on how you and your family like to eat. It's not going to hurt my feelings; you already bought the book. Now, take all those onions, carrots, and celery you chopped, fill a couple of pots with water, throw the veggies in, simmer for a couple of hours, and strain it. You just learned how to chop and how to make vegetable broth.

LESSON 3:
STEP OUTSIDE YOUR COMFORT ZONE

Spices are essential to my "outer-boro eclectic" cooking style. I was lucky enough to grow up in a Brooklyn before hipsters, when it was like a more dangerous Epcot Center filled with immigrants from Italy, Ireland, Jamaica, China, Greece, Trinidad, Egypt, Cuba, The Philippines, Israel, Puerto Rico, Russia, and their first-generation rugrats. A kid could bike over to a friend's house for dinner and—if he didn't have his bike stolen on the way there—have a culinary adventure.

Variety is the spice of life. Actually, spices are the spice of life. They're a great way to add calorie-free flavor to starchy basics, and they make lackluster vegetables shine. So try them all, even the weird ones. Discover the ones you like best and use them in unexpected ways. Put ginger, garlic, chili pepper, and cream Makhani sauce on spaghetti. Coat broccoli in cumin-spiced falafel. Spike your tomato sauce with Chinese Five Spice. Why not? Life is too short to eat boring food.

YOU'RE GONNA NEED SOME STUFF: A COMPREHENSIVE LIST

In the interest of saving you time and money, here's everything you need to ready your kitchen for the next-level cooking you're about to do.

I know it looks like a lot of stuff, but don't panic. You probably have many of these items already, but I'm not the kind of guy who makes assumptions. When I worked as a private chef, I met a surprising number of people who used their stoves to store wine bottles.

IN THE SPICE RACK

- **Adobo all-purpose seasoning:** Goya's salty spice blend.
- **Kosher or coarse salt:** It doesn't have to be blessed by a rabbi, but it needs to be coarse.
- **Ground black pepper**
- **Crushed red pepper flakes:** If you can find it, try upgrading to the smoky *Urfa bieber* (that's Turkish smoked red pepper).
- **Ground cumin:** Are you really going to toast and grind your own cumin seeds? I think we both know the answer to that.
- **Ground turmeric:** Street name, "Broke-ass Saffron."=
- **Smoked or Spanish paprika:** This smoky flavor enhancer is a kitchen MVP.
- **Hot paprika:** It has a mild spice level that won't freak out plain-Jane palates. If you're a hot-food hero, add more to build the heat.
- **Truffle salt:** I know truffle salt is overhyped, overdone, and isn't even made of real truffles. (Sad, but true. Google it.) But it's so damn delicious. And yes it's expensive, but suck it up. I just saved you thirty grand on culinary school, you ingrate.

- **Ground cinnamon:** WTF are you gonna do with a cinnamon stick?
- **Dried thyme:** This evergreen herb is great to have around because it makes whatever it touches taste kind of French. Not in a nihilistic Parisian way, though, but from Brittany or the Languedocian hills.
- **Dried oregano:** Babies born in Italy receive a jar of this pizza herb at birth.
- **Curry powder:** That jerk Christopher Columbus sailed halfway around the world (in the wrong direction) on a quest for curry. It's that good.
- **Garam masala:** This mild Indian spice blend with cumin, coriander, cardamom, cinnamon, cloves, and nutmeg—tastes like Thanksgiving.
- **Chinese five spice:** It's the garam masala of China, with Sichuan pepper, anise, fennel, cinnamon, and cloves.
- **Sugar**
- **Hot sauce:** Any kind. I like Sambal Oelek, Cholula Hot Sauce, or Sriracha.

IN THE PANTRY

- **Olive oil:** Get both kinds—use the extra virgin for salad dressings and the slutty kind for cooking.
- **Coconut oil:** Seriously, everything tastes better with a hint of coconut. Plus, you can do a lot more than cook with it. There's an entire subreddit devoted to the endless ways coconut oil can improve your life. It's a great moisturizer, hair detangler, antibacterial cream, even rust remover. Head down the rabbit hole at reddit.com/r/coconutoil.
- **Canola oil:** Great for frying.
- **Sesame oil:** This isn't for cooking. It's a finishing oil; drizzle it on or use in a dressing or sauce.
- **Vinegars:** Red wine, white wine, balsamic, rice, champagne…get one of each.
- **Honey:** As always, local is best, but the kind in the bear will do. If you're vegan or just curious, try molasses, date syrup, or maple syrup (my favorite).
- **Mustard:** Graduate from the squeeze bottle. Dijon works best in salad dressings.
- **Tahini:** This sesame paste is underutilized— you pretty much only see it on falafel, but it tastes good on anything. Even ice cream.
- **Peanut butter:** The creamy kind tastes best and the natural kind is healthiest. Try to find one that's both, like Peanut Butter & Co. Smooth Operator. Almond butter is nice to have around, too. Just saying.

- **A few types of nuts:** Almonds, cashews, peanuts, walnuts, pine nuts, and pecans. Sliced, halved, slivered, chopped. The world is your pistachio shell.
- **Seeds:** Hemp, chia, sunflower, and sesame all provide a nutritious crunch.
- **Dried fruit:** Raisins, apricots, dates, and Craisins are great ways to add a little sweetness.
- **Canned tomatoes:** There's nothing better than a freshly picked tomato, but prime tomato season is only a few weeks a year. Canned tomatoes are picked and canned during that time, so buy those to use when your grocery store only has pale orange tomatoes that taste like nothing. I always keep a few giant cans of San Marzano or plum tomatoes, and a few small cans of crushed tomatoes around.
- **Canned beans:** Kidney beans, fava beans, chickpeas, black beans, black-eyed peas, green peas—they each have their own flair.
- **Starches:** Pasta, rice, quinoa, farro, oats, barley. You have your favorites, but every now and then, branch out and try something new.
- **Vegetable broth:** Keep a couple of quarts in the pantry, and use broth instead of water when cooking grains. It makes a huge difference in flavor.

IN THE FRIDGE

- **Salad greens:** Spinach, kale, arugula, and romaine are all great options. Iceberg lettuce doesn't count.
- **Eggs:** There's some global controversy about whether you need to refrigerate eggs. The answer varies depending on how chicken farmers in different countries clean them, but, long story short, if you live in the USA (or Scandinavia, Japan, or Australia), yes.
- **Fruit preserves/jam:** A touch of strawberry or raspberry jam is an easy way to kick up a vinaigrette.
- **Olives:** Black, green, Kalamata. They're all good, except the cheap kind with the red-pepper pimientos.
- **Capers:** Did you know that a caper is a pickled flower bud?
- **Good cheese:** There is no reason a Kraft single should ever darken your fridge's deli door. Keep some gorgonzola, Parmigiano-Reggiano, feta, or Pecorino Romano around. Sure, it's more expensive, but good cheese is potent so a little goes a long way.
- **A squeeze tube of tomato paste**
- **A squeeze tube of wasabi paste**
- **Soy sauce:** What's the difference between soy sauce and shoyu? Shoyu is the Japanese term for soy sauce, and is also used to indicate that it's been fermented naturally. So all shoyu is soy sauce but not all soy sauce is shoyu.
- **Fresh herbs:** Whatever looks good at the market. Man cannot live on dried herbs alone.
- **Meat alternatives:** Try tempeh, seitan, and tofu. They all have different ingredients, textures, and flavors. See which one speaks to you.

IN THE FREEZER

- **Frozen veggies:** Frozen peas, green beans, and butternut squash are especially awesome, as is spinach. Buy a giant bag of the store brand for two bucks, and when you sauté it, the spinach won't wilt away to nothing. You'd have to spend ten times as much on fresh spinach for the same yield.
- **Meat substitutes:** I like Morningstar products best, especially the crumbles, which can help give sauces a satiating heft. Go beyond the basic veggie burger and try Quorn and Beyond Meat, too.

- **Frozen fruit:** Use for smoothies.
- **Leftover tomato sauce:** Pour it over rice, potatoes, or noodles, or poach some eggs in it for a quick shakshuka (see page 66).
- **Onions, garlic, herbs:** Pre-chop them and store in separate airtight bags so you don't have to interrupt your kitchen flow when inspiration strikes.
- **Leave room for dessert:** DIY ice cream and frozen yogurt. (See the recipes on pages 214 to 215) and stick it to Big Ice Cream.

IN THE KITCHEN CABINETS

- **Chef's knife and sharpener:** This workhorse is the only knife you really need.
- **Misto sprayer:** For misting cooking oils
- **Big 8- to 12-quart stockpot:** For making soups and boiling pasta
- **Medium saucepan**
- **Big nonstick frying pan:** Use it instead of a 200-pound cast-iron skillet that's a pain in the ass to clean.
- **Medium frying pan:** for all your sautéing needs
- **Mixing bowls:** small, medium, and large
- **Mason jars:** You don't need a Pinterest account's worth—just a few for making and storing salad dressing.
- **Giant salad bowl:** The bigger the bowl, the easier it is to toss your salad.
- **Baking sheets:** You don't need more than two.
- **Parchment paper**
- **Aluminum foil**
- **Vegetable peeler:** I like ceramic ones, or the classic in Kisag Swiss stainless steel.
- **A four-sided box grater:** for grating, slicing, shredding, or thin, mandoline-like cuts.
- **A good blender or food processor:** If you can afford it, buy a Vitamix high-performance blender that will outlast you.
- **Whisk:** A hand mixer is nice to have, too, but it's your call.
- **A cheap immersion blender:** Don't spend more than $40.
- **A nonslip cutting board:** You don't want it sliding around on you.
- **Wooden spoons**
- **A floppy spatula**
- **Set of measuring cups and spoons:** Buy two. These things get lost like socks.
- **A large strainer**
- **A colander**
- **Tongs:** the regular metal kind
- **Tupperware:** Fill all the rest of your cabinet space with these. You'll thank me when you're swimming in leftovers.

THE CONSPIRACY IS REAL

I'm sorry, but The Cookbook-Industrial Complex has been lying to you your whole life. Here are some hard truths:

1. It takes one hour to properly roast garlic. Almost every recipe says 30 minutes, and they're all pushing Rachael Ray's agenda.

2. Don't bother making your own pasta. Unless you do it for a living in an Italian mountain town, the dried box version will always be better than your kitchen art project. When you make pasta, it's inconsistent. The ends are too hard or the middle is too soft. When Ronzoni makes it, it comes out perfect every time . . . as long as you boil it in salty water for 2 minutes less than the box says, and finish in your own sauce.

3. Your crudités is dull and unappetizing. That's because your broccoli needs blanching, which is like the vegetable version of using a color-enhancing filter. Boil it in salty water for 1 minute, and then shock it in a bowl of cold water. Now it's a vibrant, restaurant green.

4. Garlic powder is the universal symbol of bad cooking in a shaker jar. It takes less than a minute to mince some garlic, and another 3 to sauté it. That's totally worth it. (Sensitive to residual garlic odor on your hands? Keep a cheap box of disposable latex gloves under the sink for stink-free mitts.)

5. You don't have to always use dried beans when you cook. Sure, if you want to use dried beans, go ahead, but get ready because you need to soak them overnight and spend hours simmering them until they aren't hard as pebbles. Can I save you a little time? Just buy canned beans. Give

them a quick rinse before using and most varieties are just fine. We're not going to be making cassoulet or cooking white beans with sage and olive oil in a flask in the dying embers of our fireplace.

6. Source ethical eggs. The idea is that happy chickens make better-tasting eggs, but who really knows if a chicken is delighted with its life? This way, at the very least, you'll feel confident that it wasn't debeaked and enslaved in a tiny cage. Download the Certified Humane app and use the money I saved you on knives towards cruelty-free eggs.

7. Cook with dried herbs and finish with fresh herbs. If you're simmering a sauce with fresh basil or cilantro, you're doing it wrong. Fresh herbs go limp and lose flavor during the cooking process. Make the sauce, *and then*

hit it with the freshness at the last second for a punch of flavor.

8. Press your damn tofu. Before you cook with tofu out of the package, you're going to want to press the water out of it if you want it to taste good. An hour or so before you use it in a recipe, cut your block of tofu into 4 slices, wrap it in a towel, and put something heavy on top like plates or books. Leave it for an hour. This will drain the water.

9. When I say "salty water" in a recipe, I mean salty like the tears you cried when Hodor held the door (or when Old Yeller died . . . if you're not a *Game of Thrones* fan.) Think ocean water in your mouth at the beach. This will improve the taste and color of what you're boiling or blanching.

1

VEGETABLES YOUR MOM RUINED

This is not a chapter full of "Yo Momma" jokes. I love moms, and not just the MILF-y ones. Your mom had the hardest job in the world—raising you, in addition to the million other things she had to take care of. (Imagine how awful it must have been to spend all that time with you, but a version of you that didn't know how to do anything yet.)

Mama tried. Before kids just dicked around on their phones all day, she had to chase your ass all over the neighborhood and get dinner on the table before the prime-time TV started. She was a woman of her time—the Food Network didn't exist yet and people still believed iceberg lettuce counted as "greens"—and you were a picky little brat who hated eating vegetables. In fairness to you, Mom likely didn't have the time, energy, and interest to crank out creative, veg-centric spreads every night that would foster a love of produce that stayed with you until adulthood. Maybe she just opened a can of peas and microwaved them in salty water. Maybe she boiled the flavor out of everything and thought butter was a spice. And there are some vegetables that are so icky, they're beyond saving—turnips, fennel, cooked carrots. Here's the thing, though. What if I told you that you don't hate these vegetables? What if I told you that it was just your mom's cooking? Yo! :: Minds blowing ::

BRUSSELS SPROUTS: VEGETABLE PUBLIC ENEMY #1

Every kid tried to make these disappear into their dinner napkin because they looked like tiny cabbages and made the whole house smell like farts. I don't want to hear anyone tell me that they don't like Brussels sprouts ever again. In researching this book, that's all I heard—your mom boiled up some sprouts and, if you were lucky, hit them with a little S&P. They were soggy, mushy, stinky, and really managed to fire up the gag reflex. Let's "un-fuck" Brussels sprouts once and for all.

What your mom didn't know is that roasting Brussels sprouts not only makes them edible, it'll make them one of your favorite vegetables. Here are a few recipes to take them to the next level.

BADASS BALSAMIC BRUSSELS SPROUTS

*Vegan

1. Preheat the oven to 400°F. Line a baking sheet with parchment paper.

2. Wash your sprouts well. Remove the tough outer leaves, trim the stems, and cut each sprout in half lengthwise.

3. Put the sprouts in a bowl. Add the olive oil and toss until the sprouts are well coated. Add the salt, black pepper, red pepper flakes, and balsamic vinegar and toss to combine.

4. Place the Brussels sprouts on the lined baking sheet, cut side down. Don't crowd them like a Japanese subway car. Roast in the preheated oven for 20 minutes.

5. Pull the baking sheet from the oven and flip the sprouts cut side up. Return to the oven and roast for another 15 minutes.

6. Some sprouts should be deep brown and crispy—almost oven-fried. Others will be caramelized and slightly crispy. I don't know what kind of oven you're working with, so if they don't look like the picture, give them a couple more minutes until they do.

7. Sprinkle with truffle salt. Serve and eat while hot—cold Brussels sprouts are nasty.

1½ pounds Brussels sprouts
1 tablespoon olive oil
Punch of kosher salt (like a pinch, but bigger. See Brasco, Donnie.)
Punch of ground black pepper
Pinch of crushed red pepper flakes
1 tablespoon balsamic vinegar
Truffle salt

#BASIC BRUSSELS SPROUTS: The very least you can do—and still have awesome sprouts—is drizzle them with a little olive oil, hit them with salt and pepper, toss them on a baking sheet, and roast at 400°F for 30 minutes.

BRUSSELS SPROUTS WITH APPLES & DATES

Things sure have changed a lot recently. First we went from a boob-based society to a butt-based one; then, after years of boring, boiled, homemade Brussels sprouts, every restaurant chose to add a killer sprout dish to their menu. Sure, most of them cheat and use bacon or lardons, a fistful of salt, and more oil than Saudi Arabia pumps in a year to make them palatable, but at least they're on the menu. Since I care about you and your health more than restaurant chefs do, let's try it in a vegan recipe that's still fucking delicious.

---

1 head garlic

¾ cup apple juice

2 tablespoons olive oil

2 tablespoons pure maple syrup

2 pounds Brussels sprouts, stems trimmed, outer layer removed, halved lengthwise

Kosher salt and ground black pepper

2 apples

5 dates, diced

½ cup roasted peanuts

1. Preheat the oven to 400°F. Line a baking sheet with parchment paper.

2. Slice the garlic head in half, crosswise. Splash with a bit of olive oil and sprinkle with salt. Put the halves back together and wrap the head of garlic in aluminum foil. Toss the packet in the oven while it's preheating.

3. In large bowl, whisk the apple juice with the olive oil and maple syrup until combined. Add the Brussels sprouts and a punch of salt and pepper. Make sure the sprouts are evenly coated.

4. Place the sprouts on the lined tray, cut side down. Pour any additional sauce over the top, as evenly as you can.

5. Roast the sprouts in the preheated oven for 40 minutes, or until they're crispy and kind of charred. I don't know what kind of oven you have, so it might take a bit more time. Be patient—you want that color and crunch. When they're done, pull the garlic out, too.

6. Thinly slice your apples.

7. Combine the sprouts, apple, dates, and peanuts in a bowl. Squeeze the roasted garlic into the bowl. Mix well and serve hot.

SESAME-TAMARI SPROUTS

I never considered serving grapes with Brussels sprouts until I tried the amazing sweet-and-savory version at Ilili in NYC—they also contained yogurt, which seems like the work of a madman. Instead, I dialed up the sweetness of the grapes with sweet potatoes and maple syrup to give it a Japanese flavor profile.

---

1 pound Brussels sprouts, stems trimmed, tough outer leaves removed, halved lengthwise

1 sweet potato, cut into half-moons (Yams work, too. I bet you couldn't tell the difference with a gun to your head.)

¼ cup tamari (or soy sauce)

¼ cup sesame oil

1 tablespoon maple syrup

¼ cup rice vinegar

2 cups red seedless grapes, halved

½ cup roasted peanuts

1. Preheat the oven to 400°F. Line a baking sheet with parchment paper.

2. Put the Brussels sprouts and sweet potatoes in a large bowl.

3. In a small bowl, whisk together the tamari, sesame oil, maple syrup, and rice vinegar. Pour the mixture over the sprouts and potatoes, making sure to coat them evenly.

4. Arrange the sprouts, cut side down, and the sweet potato half-moons on the lined sheet. Pour any leftover dressing in the bowl over the veggies.

5. Roast in the preheated oven for 35-ish minutes; your kitchen will smell like roasted sesame. You want the sprouts to be charred and crispy and the sweet potatoes to be cooked through.

6. Place the grapes and nuts in a bowl. Add the still-hot Brussels sprouts and potatoes to the bowl. Mix it up, and you're done.

NUTTY BRUSSELS SPROUTS SALAD WITH COCONUT VINAIGRETTE

*Vegan

Today's Zen practice for the day is peeling every individual leaf off of your Brussels sprouts. The payoff isn't enlightenment; it's an insanely good salad.

---

1. Bring ¼ cup of water and a pinch of salt to a boil in a saucepan. Set up a bowl of ice water.

2. Throw the sprout leaves in to blanch. Cover and cook over high heat for 2 to 3 minutes until they're bright green.

3. Drop the leaves into the bowl of ice water to shock. Remove with a slotted spoon, and pat dry with a clean towel.

4. Heat the coconut oil in a small saucepan over medium-high heat until liquefied, then continue to heat for 1 minute more.

5. Pour the hot coconut oil into a bowl. Add the olive oil, lemon juice, raisins, and olives and season with salt to taste. Mix well. Add the leaves and toss to dress. Sprinkle with the nuts and seeds and gently toss to distribute. Add red pepper flakes to taste. Eat immediately.

1 pound Brussels sprouts, stems trimmed, halved, and all leaves individually peeled

Pinch of kosher salt, plus more as needed

2 teaspoons coconut oil

1 teaspoon olive oil

Juice of 1 lemon

¼ cup raisins

¼ cup black olives, sliced

⅓ cup pine nuts, lightly toasted in the oven at 350°F or in a dry pan over medium heat

1 tablespoon shelled pistachios (you can substitute pumpkin or sunflower seeds)

Crushed red pepper flakes

CAULIFLOWER AND BROCCOLI

All kids are born knowing three things: Monsters are real, farts are hilarious, and broccoli is gross. But what the hell do kids know, anyway? Broccoli is actually awesome, and cauliflower isn't just a white version of it—they both have fiber and vitamins, and their reputation for flatulation is undeserved.

WHOLE ROASTED CAULIFLOWER

There are a zillion people out there roasting cauliflower right now. It's a revolution because cauliflower has been "crucifered" for the sins of bad cooks past, but it's worth resurrecting and a lot of talented chefs are starting to do just that. Cauliflower florets are cute, but there's a real wow factor to keeping a cauliflower intact, coating it with spices, and carving it up at the table like a Thanksgiving turkey. (Plus, it's so easy . . . so damn easy.)

2 garlic cloves, minced

Juice of 1 lemon

1 teaspoon ground cumin

1 teaspoon finely grated lemon zest

1 teaspoon ground turmeric

½ teaspoon kosher salt

2 tablespoons olive oil

1 head cauliflower, green stuff trimmed

1. Preheat the oven to 400°F.

2. Whisk all ingredients except cauliflower together in a bowl until combined.

3. Place cauliflower in a baking dish and coat with the dressing. Cover the whole thing until it looks like a yellow brain.

4. Roast in the preheated oven for about 1 hour. Start checking it around 45 minutes. You want it golden brown, not burned.

5. Cut it victoriously and serve.

CAULIFLOWER RISOTTO THAT TASTES MORE LIKE RISOTTO THAN CAULIFLOWER

I'm not easily impressed, but I impressed the hell out of myself with this dish. Even my wife, who has never been impressed by anything, said, "I can't believe this is cauliflower. It's amazing. Other people would love this." Low-carb people, you're welcome. Vegans, you can get in on this—just use nutritional yeast in place of cheese and Smart Balance and truffle salt or oil in place of truffle butter. You're welcome, too.

1. Coat the bottom of a large saucepan with olive oil. Place over medium-high heat. Add the garlic, shallots, and a pinch of salt. Stir to coat and sauté for 3 minutes until fragrant and translucent.

2. Add the mushrooms and the cauliflower and stir to combine. Add the wine and cook for 3 minutes, stirring frequently, until the cauliflower reduces in volume and the wine evaporates.

3. Add the capers, pine nuts, and broth. Stir vigorously and cook for 3 minutes. Increase the heat to high.

4. Stir in the cheese and truffle butter. Stirring vigorously, cook for 2 minutes until the broth evaporates and the cheese and butter have melted in. It should be rice-like, but not mushy. (If for some reason you messed up and it's watery, don't worry, just drain the excess liquid; you're still good.)

5. Crack some pepper over it and season with salt. Taste and adjust the salt and pepper. If you want to make it even more "truffle-y," give it a hit of truffle salt and stir.

6. Make it pretty with a couple of parsley leaves.

Olive oil
2 garlic cloves, minced
3 shallots, diced
Pinch of kosher salt, plus more as needed
8 ounces portobello mushrooms, chopped (or use baby bella mushrooms)
1 head cauliflower, grated on the large holes of a box grater so that it looks kind of like rice
¼ cup white wine
1 teaspoon capers
¼ cup pine nuts, toasted in the oven at 350°F for 10 minutes, or in a dry pan over medium heat
¼ cup vegetable broth
½ cup grated Parmigiano-Reggiano cheese
2 tablespoons truffle butter (Make the effort to use the real thing, or face the consequences.)
Ground black pepper
Truffle salt (optional)
Fresh parsley leaves for garnish

SICILIAN CAULIFLOWER SALAD

Sicilian food is some of the best in the world. The island of Sicily lies just a few miles from North Africa and has been invaded by everyone from the Greeks and Normans to the Moors over the centuries. The result is an amazing cuisine that tastes like the best of Morocco and Italy. Perfect for cauliflower!

1. Bring a pot of salty water to a boil. Add the cauliflower and boil for 3 minutes. Drain and set aside.

2. Place a large frying pan over medium heat. Add the pine nuts. Heat and shake for 3 to 5 minutes until toasty.

3. Once the pine nuts are toasty, add enough olive oil to cover the bottom of the pan and swish it around. Add the garlic, raisins, olives, capers, red pepper flakes, and tomato paste to the pan. Cook, stirring, until the garlic is fragrant.

4. Add the cauliflower and coat with the pan sauce. Cook over medium heat for 5 minutes, stirring occasionally.

5. Remove from the heat and let the cauliflower come to room temperature. Add the orange segments.

6. Refrigerate the salad in a covered container for at least 4 hours. (Overnight is better.)

7. Serve it cold with some good bread.

1 large head of cauliflower, cut into florets (It's not an art project, just cut it.)

¼ cup pine nuts

Olive oil

2 garlic cloves, minced

¼ cup raisins

½ cup green olives

1 tablespoon capers

Pinch of crushed red pepper flakes

2 tablespoons tomato paste

2 blood oranges, segmented (Use regular oranges if you have 'em.)

SPICY CAULIFLOWER FRIED "RICE"

Any idiot can grate some cauliflower, steam it a little, and try to pass it off as rice. You're not fooling or impressing anybody with that sandy mess. It takes a special kind of idiot like me to take it one step further, spice it up, and turn it into something you'd choose to eat on purpose. I'm not going to say that this tastes exactly like fried rice. It's more like the best couscous you've ever had.

2 cups frozen edamame, shelled

Canola oil

2 tablespoons minced garlic

1 bunch scallions, chopped

1 cup whole almonds

2 heads cauliflower, pulsed in a food processor, or grated, until it looks like rice

1½ teaspoons Chinese five-spice powder

½ teaspoon ground ginger

2 tablespoons chili sauce (Sriracha works)

Kosher salt

Soy sauce (optional)

1. Bring a small pot of salty water to a boil. Add the edamame and cook for 4 minutes. Drain and reserve.

2. Coat the bottom of a large frying pan with canola oil and place over medium heat. Add the garlic, scallions, and almonds. Stir and cook for 3 minutes until fragrant.

3. Add the cauliflower, five-spice powder, ginger, chili sauce, and salt to taste. Stir to combine everything. Cook for 2 minutes.

4. Cover the pan, lower the heat, and let cook for 6 minutes more.

5. Taste and adjust salt if needed.

6. Feel free to add soy sauce . . . if that's your thing. I like it better without.

PARMESAN-CRUSTED ROASTED BROCCOLI

What if broccoli and fried chicken had a delicious vegetarian baby? You would manage to do the impossible: get super excited about broccoli.

1. Preheat the oven to 400°F. Set up a bowl of ice water. Line a baking sheet with parchment paper.

2. Bring a large pot of very salty water to a boil.

3. Blanch the broccoli crowns in the boiling water for 4 minutes, then transfer them to the bowl of ice water to shock them (to set the color and halt the cooking). Once cool, drain the broccoli in a colander.

4. In a small bowl, combine the cheese, bread crumbs, egg, oil, salt, and pepper until it forms a paste.

5. Place the broccoli on the lined baking sheet. Spread the paste over the broccoli; you don't have to cover the whole thing.

6. Roast for 30 minutes.

7. Let cool. Serve, and completely change the way you think about broccoli.

2 broccoli crowns/heads, stems removed, cut into small pieces (Save the stems for a slaw. We don't waste food here.)

½ cup grated Parmiagiano-Reggiano cheese

½ cup panko bread crumbs

1 large egg

Glug of olive oil

Punch (not a pinch) of kosher salt

Generous amount of ground black pepper

EGGPLANT AND VEGGIE BALLS

Dude, do those vegetarian meatballs taste like real meatballs? Hell no they don't. Meatballs are half-assed hamburgers, and ground beef has poop in it. These are stand-alone delicious and filling, perfect for when you're entertaining carnivores or Fridays during Lent.

1 head broccoli, florets only (save the stalks for a slaw)

1 large eggplant, peeled and chopped, large dice

1 cup bread crumbs

1 cup grated mozzarella cheese

2 large eggs

1 teaspoon adobo seasoning

1 teaspoon smoked paprika

2 tablespoons chili sauce (Sriracha, Sambal, or any kind of hot sauce works here)

2 teaspoon ground cumin

1. Fill a large pot with salty water and bring it to a boil. Add the broccoli and boil for 2 minutes until it's super green, like Chinese take-out broccoli. Remove the broccoli with a slotted spoon, transfer to a cutting board, and mince.

2. Keep the water in the pot boiling and add the eggplant. Boil for 20 minutes. Drain and mash.

3. In a large bowl, combine the minced broccoli, mashed eggplant, and the remaining ingredients. Stir to combine. The hot eggplant should melt the cheese. Refrigerate the mixture for 30 minutes.

4. Preheat the oven to 400°F. Line a baking sheet with parchment paper and spray it with cooking spray or use your Misto sprayer filled with oil.

5. Using an ice cream scoop (or whatever the hell you want), form the balls. Place them on the prepared baking sheet and bake for 30 minutes. Check them out. If they're golden brown and kind of crispy, they're done. If not, give them a few more minutes.

THE GREEN INFERNO SALAD

*Vegan

Every damn ingredient in this salad is green. Your mom always said that greens were good for you, but you probably stopped trusting her when she served lima beans or acted like Tooth Fairy inflation wasn't a thing. (A quarter? Come on, ma.) Nutritionists and infographics on Pinterest back up her claim—antioxidant green vegetables provide an abundance of vitamin K, potassium, folic acid, carotenoids, and smugness.

1. Bring a pot of very salty water to a boil.

2. Cut the florets from the broccoli stalks. Blanch them in the boiling water for 2 minutes, then run cold water over them to stop the cooking process.

3. Don't throw the raw broccoli stems away. Wash them well, and using a cheese grater or a food processor, turn those stems into a slaw.

4. In a large bowl, combine the florets, slaw, olives, peas, pistachios, cucumbers, and apples. Season with salt and pepper.

5. In a small bowl, whisk together the olive oil, rice vinegar, lime juice, and agave.

6. Dress the salad and toss until it's evenly mixed. Taste and adjust the seasoning if needed.

7. Sprinkle the avocado pieces on top.

1 large head broccoli

½ cup sliced green olives

2 cups cooked peas

½ cup shelled pistachios

2 large cucumbers or 6 small ones, sliced

2 green apples, cored and sliced

Kosher salt and ground black pepper

2 tablespoons extra-virgin olive oil

⅓ cup rice vinegar

Juice of 1 lime

1 teaspoon agave nectar

1 avocado, peeled, pitted, and diced

BROCCOLI RABE WITH VEGAN SAUSAGE

I dislike vegan/vegetarian versions of [insert popular meat-based dish here] as much as movie remakes and that thing where bands replace the lead singer. (*Planet of the Apes* with Mark Wahlberg; Judas Priest without Rob Halford.) They're always sad attempts to replicate a dish you used to enjoy that end up destroying any fond memories you once had. This dish stands on its own—my own parents couldn't tell the difference. I call that the The AC/DC Exception to the Rule.

1 bunch broccoli rabe

8 ounces rotini pasta

Olive oil

2 links vegan Italian sausage (I like Field Roast brand the most.)

6 garlic cloves, thinly sliced

½ teaspoon crushed red pepper flakes

Juice of ½ lemon

1 cup reserved pasta water

2 tablespoons nutritional yeast (aka Parmesan for vegans)

Kosher salt and ground black pepper

1. Bring a pot of salty water to a boil.

2. Cut off the bottom half of the broccoli stems. Blanch the broccoli rabe for 1 minute in the boiling water. Remove and run cold water over it. Keep the water in the pot boiling. (I don't know why you need to do this, but my mother and grandmother do it, so obviously it's the right way.)

3. Undercook the pasta in the boiling water for 2 minutes less than the box instructions (firmer than al dente, but not rock hard). Reserve 1 cup of the pasta water before discarding.

4. Coat the bottom of a large sauté pan with olive oil, turn the heat to medium-high, add the sausage, and cook until brown.

5. Add the broccoli rabe and stir to coat with the oil. Lower the heat, cover the pan, and cook for 5 minutes more.

6. Add the garlic, red pepper flakes, and lemon juice to the pan. Increase the heat and sauté until the garlic becomes fragrant, about 5 minutes.

7. Add the pasta, ½ cup of the reserved pasta water, and the nutritional yeast to the pan. Mix the ingredients to combine and stir until a sauce forms, about 2 minutes. Add a mini glug of olive oil and salt and black pepper to taste.

AVOCA-INSPIRED BROCCOLI
WITH TAHINI AND HAZELNUTS

I discovered this salad at the Avoca Mill in County Wicklow, Ireland. It's one of the world's oldest manufacturing companies still in business. There was a tour of the old-school operation where throws and blankets were made by adorable little old Irish ladies and cranky weavers with looms, but the best part was the kick-ass cafeteria. It's not every day that you have a delicious bite of food—in Ireland—that inspires you to go home and make something similar, but this crushed the bland-food stereotype. There are eight Avoca Cafés in Ireland. Let's hope they open a few at their U.S. stores.

1. Preheat the oven to 350°F.

2. Place the hazelnuts on a baking sheet and roast in the oven for 8 minutes. Don't let them burn.

3. Bring a pot of salty water to a boil. Blanch the broccoli in the boiling water for 2 minutes. Remove and run cold water over it until it has completely cooled. Drain and transfer to a bowl.

4. Using a food processor, mix together the tahini, water, lemon juice, and agave until they form a dressing.

5. Add the apples and nuts to the bowl with the broccoli. Dress and mix well.

$\frac{1}{3}$ **cup hazelnuts, unpeeled**

1 large head of broccoli, cut into florets

$\frac{1}{3}$ **cup tahini**

$\frac{1}{3}$ **cup water**

Juice of 1 lemon

1 teaspoon agave nectar (maple or date syrup work, too)

1 apple, sliced

SIDE PIECES:
LET'S NOT
MAKE THEM THE
SECRET SHAME OF
EVERY DINNER

SPICY CARROT SIDE PIECE

Some vegetables get all the love, but here we honor the side pieces. The ones who have to settle for celebrating Valentine's Day on a random night that's convenient for the other person; the half-price-chocolate getters, the 99-cent-store balloon recipients. Like carrots, side pieces might not be as sexy as the main dish, but if you dress it up right and make it spicy, it'll rock you harder.

---

1. Preheat the oven to 400°F. Line a baking sheet with parchment paper.

2. In a medium bowl, whisk together all the ingredients except for the carrots until they form a paste.

3. Coat and rub the carrots with the spicy paste.

4. Place the carrots on the lined baking sheet. Drizzle the remaining spice mixture on top.

5. Bake in the preheated oven for 15 minutes, rotate the carrots, and bake for another 15 minutes. They should be tender, but not mushy.

6. Don't just throw it on the plate. Make an effort to sex it up. What's the point of a new side piece that doesn't excite you?

2 tablespoons olive oil

2 teaspoons garlic paste (or 2 garlic cloves, minced)

1 tablespoon ground cumin

1 teaspoon smoked paprika

¼ teaspoon cayenne pepper

1 teaspoon ground cinnamon

½ teaspoon kosher salt

10 small (but not baby) carrots, peeled

ROCKIN' MOROCCAN CARROT SALAD

"Cumin-y" with a citrus kick, this zesty side is unlike anything in your current menu (unless you grew up in Marrakesh). You can use the beta-carotene–packed salad as a starter, a side, a slaw for your sandwich, or add a scoop to your rice and beans to give it an unexpected kick.

1½ pounds carrots, grated, shredded, or julienned

1 cup walnuts, toasted in the oven at 350°F for 10 minutes, chopped

½ cup sliced green olives

1 bunch scallions, chopped

1 bunch fresh parsley leaves, chopped

1 garlic clove, minced (optional)

½ cup raisins, soaked in warm water for 10 minutes (This plumps them up.)

Juice of 1 orange

Juice of 1 lemon

½ cup olive oil

2 teaspoon ground cumin

¼ teaspoon crushed red pepper flakes

½ teaspoon smoked paprika

1 tablespoon honey

Kosher salt and ground black pepper

1. Combine the carrots, walnuts, olives, scallions, parsley, garlic, and raisins in a large bowl—preferably one with an airtight cover so you can refrigerate it later without washing extra bowls.

2. In a separate bowl, whisk together the orange juice, lemon juice, olive oil, spices, and honey into a dressing. Season to taste with salt and pepper.

3. Pour the dressing over the salad and toss until well combined. Taste and adjust the salt until it's right.

4. Cover the bowl. (God created plastic wrap for people without mixing bowls with airtight covers.) Refrigerate for at least 1 hour—this salad is always better the next day, so feel free to make it in advance.

GRILLED ASPARAGUS WITH VEGAN MISO BUTTER

*Vegan

"Asparagus: tastes great when you're eating it, smells even better when you're peeing it." If the Asparagus Council of America would just open my letters and use my slogan, asparagus would be the new kale already.

---

1. Get a grill pan hot. Coat with cooking spray, and then grill the asparagus. You'll want each stalk lightly charred and smoky, not limp and flaccid; about 3 minutes per side over medium-high heat.

2. In a small container with a cover, combine the miso, butter substitute, and soy sauce. Mix with a fork until completely combined.

3. Do that restaurant thing where you smear a little of the sauce on the bottom of the plate.

4. Lay the asparagus over it and slather with miso butter.

Cooking spray

1 bunch asparagus, peeled and trimmed

1 tablespoon miso paste (the lighter the better)

1 tablespoon vegan butter substitute (I use Olivo Coconut Spread; Earth Balance is good, too.)

2 teaspoons shoyu (or regular soy sauce)

SPICY SICHUAN GREEN BEANS
WITH TOFU

I'm borderline obsessed with the dry sautéed string beans from Grand Sichuan in New York City. Once, they put little bits of pork in there which creeped me out, so I decided to make my own non-porky version. They're crispy and hot, but not greasy. I should warn you, these are really spicy—so spicy that by just cooking them, you may feel like you're being pepper sprayed in the face. I suggest queuing up "The Heat Is On" as your sound track.

1. Place a wok or large sauté pan over high heat. Add the peanut oil and let it get very hot.

2. Meanwhile, in a small bowl, whisk together the vinegar, chili sauce, sesame oil, sugar, and soy sauce. Set aside.

3. Carefully add the string beans, tofu, and peppercorns to the hot oil. Stir-fry until lightly blistered and charred, about 5 minutes.

4. Lower the heat to medium and add the garlic, ginger, five-spice powder, and Sichuan pepper. Stir-fry for another minute or two.

5. Remove from the wok. Toss with the dressing and serve over rice.

¼ cup peanut oil (canola works, too)

2 teaspoons rice vinegar

1 teaspoon chili sauce (Sambal or Sriracha are the best.)

1 teaspoon sesame oil

1 teaspoon sugar

1 teaspoon soy sauce

1 pound string beans (Trim the ends. Nobody wants that weird tail part.)

8 ounces dried tofu, cut into medium dice

1 tablespoon Sichuan peppercorns

3 garlic cloves, minced

1 tablespoon peeled and minced fresh ginger

½ teaspoon Chinese five spice powder

½ teaspoon ground Sichuan pepper

GREEN BEANS AND ASPARAGUS WITH SHALLOT BASIL DRESSING

This is my go-to veggie dish for dinner parties and family meals, where people never think they want green beans. The dressing has richness and depth, so I'll catch people putting one or two green things on their plate to look virtuous . . . and then coming back for seconds once they've tasted it.

1 pound green beans, ends trimmed

1 bunch asparagus, tough ends trimmed

1 shallot, minced

Juice of 1 lemon

Punch of kosher salt

½ teaspoon ground black pepper

2 tablespoons honey (or maple/ date syrup)

2 tablespoons Dijon mustard

¾ cup olive oil

1 bunch fresh basil leaves

½ cup slivered almond, toasted for 10 minutes in the oven at 350°F or in a dry pan over medium heat

1. Bring a medium saucepan filled with salty water to a boil. (Just a little salty. Don't go crazy.) Add the green beans and blanch in the boiling water for 2 minutes. Remove with a slotted spoon and set aside. Blanch the asparagus for 2 minutes. Remove with a slotted spoon or tongs and set aside.

2. Add the shallot, lemon juice, salt, pepper, honey, mustard, oil, and basil to the bowl of a food processer or blender. Pulse until you have a smooth dressing.

3. Arrange the vegetables side by side on a serving plate. Pour the dressing over the still-warm vegetables and top with the almonds.

PICK-YOU-UP SMOOTHIES

HANGOVER PREVENTION SMOOTHIE: DON'T SAY I NEVER DID ANYTHING FOR YOU

*Vegan

Listen up, lushes, hangover prevention usually means taking two Tylenol and chugging a sports drink before passing out. But your liver will hate you even more for having to filter out the acetaminophen in addition to the massive quantity of alcohol. Then it's time for your body to deal with the chemicals and sugar in the Gatorade. Why are you surprised that you feel like shit?

You can do a better job with these natural ingredients and a blender—you'll get hydration and electrolytes from the coconut water, potassium from the banana, and vitamin E from the almond butter. I throw in some strawberries for vitamin C—they make it taste great, and I once read a study that said strawberries can protect the stomach from alcohol toxicity.

Make this smoothie before going out. Put it in the fridge and drink before bed. Wake up human.

Put all the ingredients in a blender. Blend for about a minute until you have a 32-ounce smoothie. Refrigerate. Shake before you pour. Drink the whole thing . . . or as much as you can.

16 ounces coconut water

1 banana

2 cups strawberries, fresh or frozen

1 heaping tablespoon almond butter

WAKE UP LITTLE SMOOTHIE, WAKE UP

When I make my morning wake-up smoothie (usually on a hot day when I'm not in the mood for a hot beverage) I might be in a cranky mood. But after I'm done with it, I'm feeling fine, and singing my smoothie song to the tune of the Everly Brothers' 1958 hit, "Wake Up Little Susie." It's basically a piña colada with caffeine instead of booze. This recipe makes a quart. You can share it with three friends, or drink the whole thing yourself.

2 cups frozen pineapple chunks

1½ cups coconut milk

1 cup cold brewed coffee or 1 ounce coffee concentrate plus 1 cup water (I like Grady's Coldbrew.)

1 tablespoon hemp seeds

2 tablespoons sugar or agave nectar

Blend all the ingredients until fully combined.

2

WHERE DO YOU GET YOUR PROTEIN FROM, BRO?

People are peculiar. They'll offer you a slice of birthday cake, or hand you a beer and a cigarette without thinking twice. It's no skin off their ass if you become a diabetic alcoholic with lung cancer. However, as soon as someone finds out you're vegan or vegetarian, they're immediately (obsessively) concerned with your protein intake. "Where do you get your protein from, bro?" they ask, eyes wide with disbelief, as though I'll suddenly dry up like a leaf and blow away unless I devour an entire steak on the spot.

First of all, have you ever met or even heard of someone with health problems related to a lack of protein? No, you haven't. That's because it's just not a thing that happens to first world people who eat a sufficient amount of calories. The FOMOP (Fear of Missing Out on Protein) seems to have originated from 1980s bodybuilding magazine lore. Need I remind you that these are the same magazines that owned the protein supplement companies that convinced a generation of young people that they needed to drink protein shakes several times a day for "growth and repair"? Look, I'm not selling anything but this book, and you're already reading it.

Wanna know where I (and you should) get my protein from? Nuts . . . and beans, and eggs, and yogurt, tofu, tempeh, seitan, quinoa, seeds, whole grains, and, when I feel like it, the occasional fake meat product or protein shake. I'm 6 foot 3 inches and 250 pounds. I'm growing and repairing just fine on a vegetarian diet. Baseball slugger Prince Fielder, tennis champion Venus Williams, MMA fighters Mac Danzig and Jake Shields, Olympic gold medalist Carl Lewis, strength coach Mike Mahler, and triathlete punk legend John Joseph all kick ass without putting meat in their mouths. And you can, too. (As long as you get enough protein.)

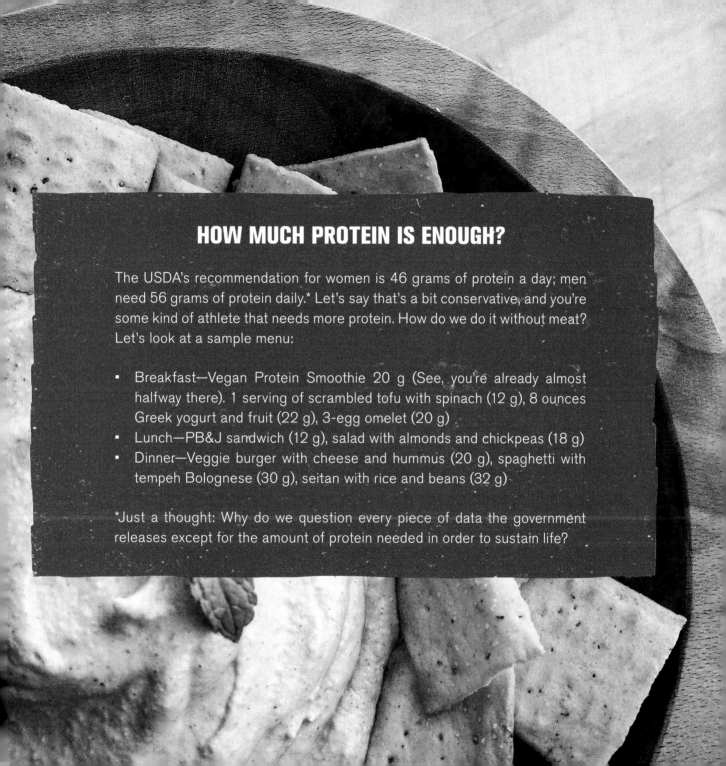

HOW MUCH PROTEIN IS ENOUGH?

The USDA's recommendation for women is 46 grams of protein a day; men need 56 grams of protein daily.* Let's say that's a bit conservative, and you're some kind of athlete that needs more protein. How do we do it without meat? Let's look at a sample menu:

- Breakfast—Vegan Protein Smoothie 20 g (See, you're already almost halfway there). 1 serving of scrambled tofu with spinach (12 g), 8 ounces Greek yogurt and fruit (22 g), 3-egg omelet (20 g)
- Lunch—PB&J sandwich (12 g), salad with almonds and chickpeas (18 g)
- Dinner—Veggie burger with cheese and hummus (20 g), spaghetti with tempeh Bolognese (30 g), seitan with rice and beans (32 g)

*Just a thought: Why do we question every piece of data the government releases except for the amount of protein needed in order to sustain life?

PEANUT BUTTER TACOS

Admit it: every vegan taco you've ever eaten tasted like nobody gave a fuck about making it. They lazily slapped some lettuce on a tortilla, maybe some guac (if you're lucky) and mock meat, then acted like that was good enough for you. Somebody needs to fix this dire vegan taco situation, and that somebody is me. You like peanut butter? Of course you do. You like Sriracha? Who doesn't? You like smoked tempeh? Hell yeah you do. You like pretty colors and mangoes? You're going to love this.

1. Preheat the oven to 350°F.

2. Place the tempeh on a baking sheet. Bake for 15 minutes.

3. Meanwhile, combine your carrots, cabbage, and mango in a large bowl with a pinch of salt.

4. In a separate smaller bowl, whisk together the Sriracha, sesame oil, and lime juice until combined.

5. Pour the dressing over the slaw, add the peanuts, and mix well. Set aside and let the flavors combine.

6. After 15 minutes, pull the tempeh out of the oven. Stack 6 tortillas, and wrap them in aluminum foil. Place them in the oven to get them taco-ready and hot, about 20 minutes.

7. Remove the hot tortillas from the oven. Spread 1 tablespoon of peanut butter on each tortilla. (The PB will get all melty and awesome. I know. I love you, too.)

8. Fill the tacos with the baked tempeh, Sriracha slaw, and some cilantro and crush 'em.

7 ounces smoked tempeh, thinly sliced (or use regular tempeh: mix up some EVOO and smoked paprika until it becomes a paste, and coat it.)

1 cup shredded carrots

1 cup shredded red cabbage

1 mango, peeled, pitted, and julienned

Pinch of kosher salt

1 tablespoon Sriracha

1 tablespoon sesame oil

Juice of 2 limes

½ cup peanuts

6 tortillas (corn, flour, or the hippie spouted kind)

6 tablespoons peanut butter

Fresh cilantro for garnish

PEANUT BUTTER HUMMUS

Like an aging movie star who gets the occasional nip and tuck to stay relevant and prolong her last "fuckable" day, hummus needs a makeover to stay in the game. But the recipe for hummus hasn't changed since Mary fed it to Jesus as baby food in the manger. Tradition is cool, but boring chip 'n' dips aren't. No worries. This peanut butter–spiked recipe will turn anyone into a card-carrying "hummusexual."

One 20-ounce can fava beans, drained and rinsed

3 tablespoons peanut butter (If you know what's good, you'll choose extra-spreadable Peanut Butter & Co. Smooth Operator.)

Juice of 1 lemon

1 garlic clove

½ cup unsweetened almond milk

1 tablespoon ground cumin

2 teaspoons kosher salt

2 tablespoons olive oil

1 teaspoon Sriracha

1 teaspoon smoked paprika, plus more for sprinkling on top

1. Combine all the ingredients in the bowl of a food processor and process until they become "hummus-y."

2. Taste for seasoning. If it needs additional seasoning (it shouldn't), add it now.

3. Using a spatula, scrape it out of the processor and into a serving bowl.

4. Sprinkle some paprika on top—if you're feeling like a fancy-pants, drop some peanuts on it.

5. Serve with toasted pita or crudités.

ELKA'S LENTIL AND RICE VEGGIE BURGER

I know a lot of world-class food people, and at the top of my list is my mother-in-law. I'm not just kissing up, either. She's easily the best cook I know and an awesome mom. An example: My wife has been a vegetarian since she was twelve, when store-bought veggie burgers used to taste like sawdust and cardboard. Her mom responded with this recipe for the best veggie burger I've ever had. Recently, I hovered around the kitchen and took precise notes to make sure I got it right. This isn't a half-assed version of a hamburger—it's a delicious, stand-alone Moroccan version of arancini. If you have people over for dinner, make this and no one will miss the meat. (It makes ten to twelve patties, so they can have seconds.)

1. Rinse the rice and lentils in a strainer, then transfer to a large saucepan over medium heat. Toast for 3 minutes, add 5 cups of water, and bring to a boil. Reduce to a simmer and set the timer for 50 minutes (you want them slightly overcooked).

2. Meanwhile, heat the olive oil in a large sauté pan over medium-high heat. Add the onion and salt and stir to combine. Cook until caramelized, about 30 minutes, stirring every 5 minutes. You'll know you're done when they're chocolate brown.

3. Add the caramelized onions (and any brown bits from the pan) to the cooked rice and lentil mix. Stir in the cheese, eggs, parsley, cumin, turmeric, salt, and pepper until the cheese has melted and the eggs are completely incorporated.

4. Allow the rice and lentil mixture to cool to room temperature.

5. In a bowl, mix the bread crumbs and cornstarch and set aside.

6. Form the rice and lentil mixture into firm patties. Dredge each patty with the bread crumb mixture until fully coated. Place the patties on a baking sheet and refrigerate for at least an hour. This can be done in advance.

1 cup short-grain rice

1 cup lentils (any kind but red)

Olive oil

3 onions, thinly sliced

Punch of kosher salt

½ cup shredded cheese (use whatever you like)

3 large eggs

¼ cup fresh parsley leaves

2 tablespoons ground cumin

1 tablespoon ground turmeric

Kosher salt and ground black pepper

2 cups bread crumbs

⅓ cup cornstarch

Canola oil for frying

7. Heat the canola oil in a frying pan over medium heat until it shimmers. Add the patties, but don't crowd them like I-405 at rush hour. Fry until golden brown on both sides, 2 to 3 minutes per side. Transfer the finished patties to a paper towel–lined plate. Repeat with the next batch.

JUST THE TIP: UPGRADE TO ISRAELI EGGPLANT PARM Follow steps 1 to 5 and preheat the oven to 350°F. Now, you're going to need 2 large eggplants, 2 eggs lightly beaten, and 2 cups of tomato sauce. Cut your eggplants into 2-inch-thick rounds, then slice each one lengthwise, stopping three-quarters of the way to the edge. (You should have eggplant rounds that open like a cheap hamburger bun or a makeup compact.) Fill them with the rice mixture. Brush each filled piece with the egg wash, and then drag through the bread crumbs and cornstarch mix until coated. Fry until golden on all sides. Lay all the eggplant pieces flat in an oven-safe baking dish, pour the tomato sauce on top, and bake for 1 hour.

DR. DEVASH'S SHAKSHUKA

Technically, shakshuka is just Middle Eastern poached eggs in a spicy tomato gravy, but that's like saying pizza is just dough with cheese and sauce. Like pizza, there's good shakshuka, awful shakshuka, and oh-my-God-this-is-awesome shakshuka. If you want to try the best, go to the Mecca (that might be the wrong word choice here) of shakshuka: The infamous Dr. Shakshuka restaurant in the old Arab port city of Jaffa, Israel. The Doctor throws down fantastic home-style Libyan food under a canopy of antique copper pans. If you're in Tel Aviv and you don't take a stroll over there, you missed something incredible.

Full disclosure: Dr. Shakshuka happens to be my father-in-law's brother-in-law. Dr. Devash, my FIL, is the coolest biotech supergenius and blues guitar player you'll ever meet. Sinatra's "My Way" should be playing wherever he goes, because he lives life—and makes eggs—his way.

Anyway, this is my version of Dr. Devash's version of Dr. Shakshuka's namesake specialty. With all these advanced-degree shakshuka wizards around, I've managed to pick up a trick or two.

---

2 tablespoons olive oil

1 large onion, cut into small dice

3 garlic cloves, sliced

1 red bell pepper, seeded and cut into small dice

2 pounds tomatoes, diced (or use a 27-ounce can of diced tomatoes if you can't find ripe ones)

¼ cup tomato paste

2 teaspoons ground cumin

1 teaspoon ground black pepper

2 teaspoons kosher salt

1 teaspoon smoked or sweet paprika

¼ teaspoon crushed red pepper flakes (or Aleppo or cayenne pepper)

2 tablespoons honey

6 large eggs

Chopped fresh parsley for garnish

1. Coat the bottom of a large skillet with olive oil and place over medium heat. Add the onion, garlic, and bell pepper and stir to coat with the oil. Cook until the mixture smells super garlicky, about 5 minutes.

2. Add the tomatoes and mash them up a bit with a fork or potato masher, then stir in the tomato paste. Let cook down for 7 minutes.

3. Add all of the spices and the honey at once. Mix thoroughly.

4. Crack your eggs right into the skillet. Spread them out evenly, giving them space to poach in the tomato mixture.

5. Lower the heat to a simmer, cover the pan, and let cook for 10 to 12 minutes. You should have beautifully poached eggs in a delicious tomato sauce.

6. Make it pretty with parsley. Serve it with pita or a baguette, or do it the Sicilian way—cook 4 ounces of dry pasta and top with the eggs and sauce.

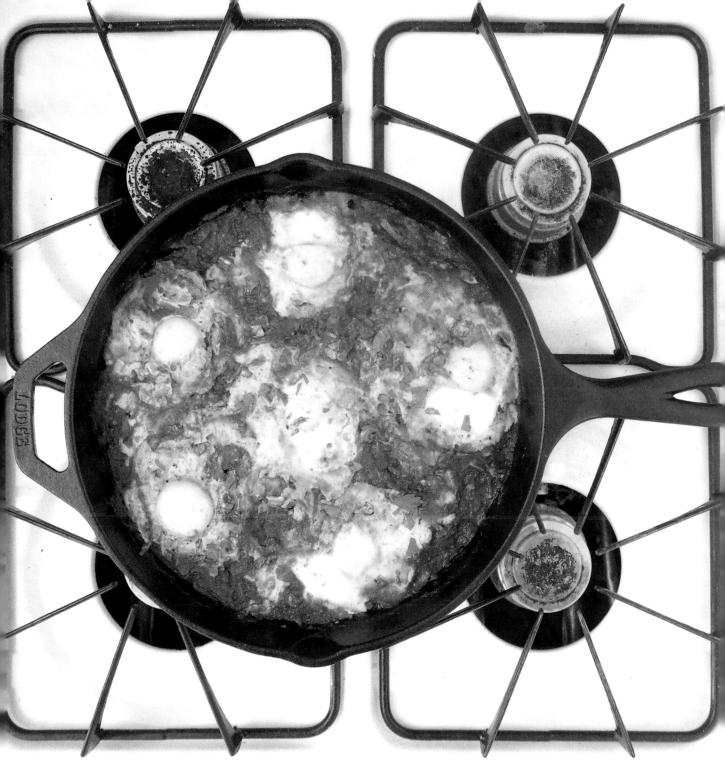

PANELLE SANGWITCH
AKA SICILIAN FALAFEL

There's a neighborhood in Brooklyn called Gravesend. I'm not making this up, it's called Grave's End. If the Mafia existed (which they totally don't), they'd probably set up shop in a place called Gravesend. And that would mean that the neighborhood would have incredible Italian food. Forget what you heard about the best Italian food in NYC. If you haven't been to Joe's of Avenue U (it's on Avenue U), you haven't had the best Italian food in New York. It's a no-frills Sicilian specialty joint. Try the panelle special (chickpea fritters on a hamburger bun with cheese heaped on); it's the best in the city, or any city outside of Palermo. Here's my version: Try this in place of your regular veggie burger.

---

2 cups water

Olive oil

1 cup chickpea flour (It's easy to find now, thanks to gluten-free people.)

1 teaspoon kosher salt

½ crushed red pepper flakes

Canola oil

1 package store-bought hamburger rolls*

1 cup ricotta cheese (You can use another cheese, but keep it soft.)

1 cup grated pecorino Romano cheese

Fresh parsley for garnish

Another Option: Feel free to serve the fritters without the bun and the cheese. These will work as an appetizer or even as a topper for salad.

1. Bring the water to a boil in a small saucepan.

2. Grease a 9 x 13-inch baking sheet with olive oil.

3. Add the chickpea flour, salt, and red pepper flakes to the boiling water. Reduce to a low simmer and whisk to combine until it becomes thick and lumpless like polenta—figure on 7 or 8 minutes of whisking and simmering.

4. Using a spatula, spread the mixture onto the prepared baking sheet in an even layer. Let it cool to room temperature. Cover it with parchment paper and refrigerate for at least 2 hours to properly set.

5. Remove the baking sheet from the fridge. Cut the firmed batter into small rectangles or triangles or ovals about 2 inches long.

6. Add the canola oil to a big frying pan until it's about ½ inch deep. Get the oil very hot and add the cutouts. Working in batches, fry until golden, about 4 minutes, rotating every minute. Repeat if needed.

7. Drain on paper towels.

8. Put a couple of fritters inside a hamburger bun. Sprinkle with a little salt and add ¼ cup of each of the cheeses. Throw some parsley on it.

DEVILS on HORSEBACK

Devils on Horseback are a cocktail party classic hors d'oeuvre that I had never heard of until I was twenty-eight years old. I guess my parents didn't throw the right kind of parties. They are sweet, savory, and smoky—what's not to like? Traditionally they're stuffed with mango chutney, but I prefer the texture of toasted pecan halves and obviously I swapped out the bacon for fakin'. I made these for a wedding once, and the crush of well-dressed people trampling each other to grab a handful looked like something out of *World War Z*.

1. Preheat the oven to 400°F. Line a baking sheet with parchment paper.

2. Slice each date lengthwise. Remove the pit and replace it with a pecan.

3. Close the date and wrap it with a tempeh strip. Use the toothpick like a sword to pierce the pecan and date in order to hold them together.

4. Place the wrapped dates on the lined baking sheet. Lightly spray them with your Misto or cooking spray.

5. Bake until the tempeh is crispy, 12 to 15 minutes. If you crank up "Sympathy for the Devil" by The Rolling Stones on repeat, it'll be ready around the time the song has played twice.

6. Remove from the oven. Serve hot, and get out of the way.

9 Medjool dates (Don't skimp and buy cheap dates—get the big, sticky ones. It makes a difference.)

1 package Lightlife Organic Fakin' Bacon Tempeh Strips (I like this brand best, but any veggie bacon is fine.)

9 pecan halves

9 toothpicks, soaked in water for 30 minutes to prevent burning

Misto filled with olive oil, or cooking spray

BAKED EGGS IN AVOCADO BOATS

Eggs, hot sauce, and cheese stuffed into an avocado boat is like a low-carb version of a breakfast burrito, or avocado toast for the kind of people who are afraid of bread. Or just, you know, people who like eating things out of boats. It's also one of those meals that looks impressive on Instagram, but is literally just cutting something in half and throwing it in the oven—and it's acceptable for breakfast, lunch, a snack, or dinner.

1. Preheat the oven to 400°F.

2. Using a spoon, widen the opening in each avocado half to accommodate the egg.

3. Crack the eggs and pour into the avocado boats (one egg per boat).

4. Hit the egg with salt and pepper.

5. Carefully place the avocado halves on a baking sheet (don't spill the egg) and bake in the preheated oven for 15 to 20 minutes.

6. Hit it with some hot sauce and cheese.

1 avocado, halved, pit removed
2 medium or large eggs
Pinch of kosher salt and ground
  black pepper
Cholula hot sauce
Grated cheese

FLUFFY TRUFFLE-Y EGGS

Once, I saw a YouTube video of someone making super-fluffy eggs and it looked awesome, but it was in Russian. I didn't understand what she was saying, but her body language made it clear that beating the hell out of egg whites was key. It wasn't rocket science to figure out the rest.

4 large eggs

1 piece lavash bread (any flat bread will do)

Pinch of truffle salt

Pinch of ground black pepper

Parmigiano-Reggiano cheese

1. Separate the egg whites from the yolks—segregate them like the 1950s South. Put the whites in a medium mixing bowl; reserve the yolks intact. Make sure no yolk is mixed in with your whites, or step three will not work.

2. Season the whites generously with truffle salt.

3. Using a hand mixer, beat the egg whites until stiff peaks develop. (Once you can turn the bowl upside down over your head and nothing falls out, you're good.)

4. Preheat the oven to 350°F.

5. Line a baking sheet with parchment paper and place the bread on top. Lift the fluffy egg whites in one big cloud and place them on top of the bread. Scoop a well into the center of the eggs so they resemble a soft, fluffy bowl.

6. Fill the well with 3 of the egg yolks and season them with truffle salt and pepper. Try not to break the yolks, but if you do, it's not the end of the world.

7. Put the baking sheet in the oven and bake for around 15 minutes. (Now, I don't know how you like your eggs or how your oven works; 15 minutes is a guideline. It might take 10 or 20 minutes for you to get your eggs the way you want them.)

8. Using a microplane, grate some cheese over it, then get a knife and fork and crack this thing open.

PARMESAN-CRUSTED SWEET POTATO AND KALE FRITTATA

The next time you're standing in front of the open refrigerator door wondering how to make a meal out of whatever's in that Tupperware and a stick of string cheese, do me a favor: make a quick assessment of what's inside, then grab a frying pan. What vegetables are starting to wilt in your produce drawer? Is that a take-out container from two nights ago? If what's in that Tupperware in back is still edible (sniff test), throw that in, too. Heat it all up, cover with a layer of beaten eggs and cheese, and then place it into the oven. Maybe use the broiler at the end if you're feeling fancy. It's like the far, far less disgusting version of dumpster diving, but in your own fridge. This is my favorite version.

---

1. Preheat the oven to 400°F.

2. In a large ovenproof sauté pan, melt the coconut oil over medium heat. Add the onion slices, yams, adobo, and tomato paste and stir to combine. Cover the pan and cook for 15 minutes, stirring occasionally.

3. Add the kale and wilt for 1 minute. Turn off the heat.

4. In a medium bowl, whisk the eggs with paprika, cumin, fenugreek, and pepper until beaten together.

5. Add the egg mixture to the onions, yams, and kale in the sauté pan. Mix well and cover the top with the cheese.

6. Bake for 30 to 40 minutes. The cheese should create a crust, and the interior should be dry when pierced by a fork.

7. Let cool for 10 minutes. Serve hot, warm, or at room temperature.

1 tablespoon coconut oil

1 huge or 2 small onions (white, yellow, red, whatever), sliced

2 sweet potatoes, washed and sliced into ½-inch rounds

2 teaspoons adobo seasoning

1 tablespoon tomato paste

1 cup baby kale (or spinach)

6 large eggs (Feel free to use one of those 16-ounce containers of egg whites or Egg Beaters to save a whole bunch of calories.)

1 tablespoon plus 1 teaspoon smoked paprika

1 teaspoon ground cumin

¼ teaspoon ground fenugreek

Pinch of ground black pepper

2 tablespoons grated Parmigiano-Reggiano cheese

SWEET PEA, AVOCADO, AND MINT HUMMUS

This is a really light version of hummus that's perfect for springtime and summer. The taste is creamy, minty, and refreshing. It's substantial, but not so substantial that it's going to weigh you down. Cut up five tortillas into quarters, mist with some cooking spray, and sprinkle with a pinch of salt. Bake them at 350°F for 10 minutes, and you have chips and dip. If you don't want chips, slice up some cucumbers instead. If you want lunch, spiralize a couple of zucchinis into noodles, and dress with the pesto. This recipe can be either hummus or pesto because it's a free country and you can call it whatever you want.

Put all the ingredients in a food processor and blend together until it's smooth. Taste and adjust the salt as needed.

2 cups frozen sweet peas, thawed

1 bunch fresh mint, washed and stemmed

1 avocado, pitted and peeled

Juice of 2 lemons

½ cup cashews

Punch of kosher salt

2 tablespoons olive oil

½ cup water

1 tablespoon tahini or nut butter

Homemade chips for serving (optional)

FRITTATA SENZA UOVA: VEGAN FRITTATA WITH DANDELION GREENS

A frittata without eggs makes about as much sense as spaghetti without pasta or chicharrones without pork; but those kinds of contradictions—like this eggless, cheeseless, but not tasteless, frittata—are what this book is all about. The star ingredient here is dandelion greens because their bitterness matches my disposition, but there's something so optimistic about seeing them at the farmers' market; it's like they're telling you, "Winter is almost over! Look at me, I'm dandelion greens. You'll be wearing short sleeves in a few weeks." (If it's the dead of winter, use spinach or move somewhere better.)

---

1. Preheat the oven to 350°F.

2. Coat the bottom of a large sauté pan with olive oil and set over medium heat. Add the onion and a pinch of the salt, and sauté for 5 minutes. Add the garlic and sauté for another 3 minutes until fragrant.

3. Add the potato, dandelion greens, tomatoes, olives, thyme, and oregano along with a pinch of salt and pepper. Stir to combine, lower the heat, and let cook for 5 minutes.

4. Meanwhile, place the tofu and nutritional yeast in a blender and blend until smooth.

5. Remove the pan from the heat and pour the contents into a lightly oiled baking dish. Pour the tofu blend over the potato and greens mixture, making sure to cover evenly. Then top the whole thing with a layer of Daiya slices.

6. Bake in the preheated oven for 45 minutes to 1 hour, or until it smells like a pizzeria.

7. Remove from the oven and let stand for 10 to 15 minutes, then serve.

Olive oil

1 onion, cut into small dice

Kosher salt and ground black pepper

2 garlic cloves, minced

1 large potato (I don't care what kind you use), cut into medium dice

1 bunch dandelion greens, bottom third removed (about 2 cups, loosely packed)

½ cup grape tomatoes

½ cup Kalamata olives, sliced

2 teaspoons dried thyme

1 tablespoon dried oregano

2 tablespoons nutritional yeast

1 pound silken tofu

4 slices Daiya nondairy cheese, provolone type

NIHILISTIC FRITTATA

This pitch-black frittata is meant to represent the darkness within (thanks to a bit of black bean sauce for color). My intention here was to appeal to Goth chicks, which is something I spent a lot of time doing in my teens and early twenties by attending Goth/industrial parties at The Bank, Batcave, and Limelight. I wasn't one to dress like a Dracula, but knew where all the hottest subculture girls hung out. (Hint: Not Sunday hardcore matinees at CBGB.) Anyway, this flavor combination is insane in a good way. Just like most Goth chicks.

Cooking oil

1 large leek, sliced (Cut it in half lengthwise and thoroughly wash the inside. Leeks are filthy.)

2 garlic cloves, minced

1 Japanese yam (or regular sweet potato), thinly sliced

12 ounces lotus root, thinly sliced

1/3 cup black bean paste

1 tablespoon chili sauce

7 large eggs

1/4 cup Bulgarian feta (Bulgarians like their cheese super salty. If that's a problem, use feta from somewhere else.)

1. Preheat the oven to 400°F.

2. Coat the bottom of an ovenproof skillet with oil and place on the stove over medium heat. Add the leeks and garlic. Cook until soft and fragrant, 3 to 5 minutes.

3. Add the yam, lotus root, black bean paste, and chili sauce and stir to coat evenly. Cover and cook for 10 minutes, stirring occasionally. Turn off the heat.

4. Scramble the eggs in a medium bowl. Pour the beaten eggs over the mixture in the skillet. Stir to combine; it should look black and slightly soupy.

5. Play some music from Dead Can Dance and dramatically crumble the feta over the top. You're totally Goth now.

6. Bake for 25 to 30 minutes until slightly crispy on the outside and completely set on the inside. Prick it with a fork to check.

RED WINE SEITAN WITH MUSHROOMS AND THYME

This is one of my favorite "Frenchified" comfort food dishes. I'm sure there's a name for it, but I'd just mangle the pronunciation, so we'll just call it what it is. The combo of red wine, butter, and thyme works together to make this 15-minute meal taste like something that took hours to make. *Allez.*

2 tablespoons butter (Vegans, use olive oil.)

1 pound seitan, chopped into bite-size pieces

¼ cup all-purpose flour

8 ounces mushrooms, sliced (baby Bella or regular old button mushrooms work)

½ cup red wine (the kind you'd drink)

1 teaspoon dried thyme

Kosher salt and ground black pepper

½ bunch parsley, chopped for garnish

1. Melt the butter in a large saucepan over medium heat and swish it around to cover the bottom of the pan.

2. Meanwhile, coat the seitan with the flour and shake off any excess.

3. Add the seitan to the saucepan and cook for 3 minutes on each side until lightly browned.

4. Add the mushrooms, wine, thyme, salt, and pepper and stir to combine well (everything should be wine colored). Cook, uncovered, until the mixture begins to bubble.

5. Lower the heat and cover the pan. Cook for 5 more minutes. Stir in the parsley, and taste. Adjust the seasoning if needed.

6. Serve over mashed potatoes or with good bread.

BAKED MOFONGO

"Healthy Mofongo" sounds like an oxymoron, like "Compassionate Conservative". Well, after you taste this, it should make more sense. I spent a week in Puerto Rico and enviously watched as my friends ate *mofongo* and had borderline religious experiences. Unfortunately I couldn't find a vegetarian version so I ate my plain *tostones* begrudgingly, but when I got home, I had my revenge. I took on the most delicious, porky, fried "plantain-y," heart-attack-on-a-plate dish, removed the meat and the fried, and kept all the awesomeness.

---

3 ripe plantains, peeled and sliced into ½-inch pieces

6 garlic cloves, peeled

2 tablespoons olive oil

8 ounces seitan, cubed

1 teaspoon adobo seasoning

1 tablespoon smoked paprika

1. Preheat the oven to 400°F. Line a baking sheet with parchment paper.

2. Toss the sliced plantains and garlic with 1 tablespoon of the olive oil, then arrange on the lined baking sheet.

3. Bake in the preheated oven for 15 minutes, then flip them and bake for another 10 minutes. The plantains should be browned on both sides, but soft inside. The garlic should be lightly browned.

4. In a medium bowl, combine the seitan with the remaining 1 tablespoon olive oil, the adobo, and paprika. Toss until the seitan is well-coated and tinted red from the paprika.

5. Heat a nonstick frying pan over medium-high heat. Add the paprika-coated seitan chunks and cook until crispy.

6. Combine the seitan, plantains, and garlic in the bowl of a food processor. Pulse until combined into a mashy texture. Say hello to your vegetarian mofongo.

7. Use a small bowl as a mold for your mofongo. Fill it to the brim, loosen with a knife around the sides, turn it upside down, and drop it onto a plate. Carefully lift the bowl for the big reveal.

8. Eat while hot.

ABOUT THE SAUCE: Add whatever you like, or do nothing—mofongo doesn't require a sauce. I like to garnish it with some chopped mango, parsley, and shallot, and squeeze fresh lemon juice on top.

NOT-FROM-A-BOX FALAFEL

*Vegan

Eating falafel made from a box is like shoving a bunch of chemicals into your mouth. You wouldn't just swallow a bunch of random chemicals if they were in pill form, would you? OK, maybe that's a bad example, but you get my point. Anyway, this isn't about Valley of the Dolls; it's about The Jordan Valley, extending from the Sea of Galilee to the Dead Sea, where falafel stands are as serious about fried chickpea balls as Neapolitans are about pizza. This is how to do it with real ingredients—you won't miss the MSG.

1. Soak your chickpeas overnight in water. Drain and rinse. DO NOT COOK THE CHICKPEAS. (Mushy falafel is gross.)

2. Measure out 2 cups of the drained chickpeas and transfer to the bowl of a food processor. (You can boil the leftovers to soften and use to make some hummus or throw them in a stew.)

3. Add all the other ingredients, except the sesame seeds and bread crumbs, to the food processor. Pulse until the ingredients combine to form a sandy-looking mixture. Think couscous, not hummus.

4. Refrigerate the mixture for 1 hour. Add the sesame seeds and bread crumbs. Mix well.

5. Place a medium saucepan over medium-high heat. Pour canola oil into the saucepan to a depth of about 2 inches. (Don't use olive oil; it has a low smoke point, so it's likely to burn, taste terrible, stink up your kitchen, and maybe give you cancer.) When the oil starts to ripple, drop a tiny piece of the mixture in as a tester. If it's bubbling and frying, you're good.

6. Form the mixture into balls using an ice cream scooper or your hands. Carefully drop your balls into the hot oil. Fry 4 falafel balls at a time for about 2 minutes on each side until golden brown. You've seen a falafel before—make it look like that. Drain on paper towels. Repeat with the remaining mixture.

7. Serve the falafel over salad with a tahini dressing, inside a pita, or just eat the balls.

1½ cups dry chickpeas
6 scallions, roughly chopped
5 garlic cloves
1 bunch fresh parsley, leaves roughly chopped
2 teaspoons flour (whatever kind you have on hand)
2 teaspoons ground cumin
2 teaspoons kosher salt
½ teaspoon crushed red pepper flakes
½ teaspoon ground turmeric
1 teaspoon baking soda
2 teaspoons sesame seeds
¼ cup bread crumbs
Canola oil for frying

TIPS

- Make the falafel balls a little bigger and press down to make veggie burger patties.

- If you want to be a hosting hero/ine, hard-boil a bunch of eggs, slice them in half, coat the egg with some of the uncooked falafel mix, and fry them for vegetarian falafel-coated Scotch eggs. Your guests will love you. Trust.

CRUNCHY ROASTED FAVA BEANS WITH CHILE AND MINT

Beans, beans, they're good for your heart. . . . So why aren't we eating more of them? It's the fart stigma, right? You think if you eat a bunch of beans you're going to have more gas than BP. Listen, one of the things I've learned is that's a myth. It only happens if your beans are undercooked. When they're properly cooked—soft on the inside with a bit of snap to the skin—they don't cause any more gastric distress than any other food. (But yes, if you eat undercooked beans, it's going to sound like the assault on Fallujah coming out of you.)

---

1 bunch fresh mint leaves

1 garlic clove

2 tablespoons olive oil

¼ cup water

2 teaspoons chili powder (sub in anything spicy here)

One 20-ounce can fava beans, drained and rinsed

Kosher salt

1. Preheat the oven to 400°F. Line a baking sheet with parchment paper.

2. Combine the mint, garlic, oil, water, and chili powder in a blender or food processor and blend until you have a pesto-like sauce.

3. Combine the beans and the sauce in a bowl. Coat the beans evenly.

4. Spread out the beans on the lined baking sheet. Sprinkle them with salt.

5. Roast in the preheated oven for 30 minutes. Test-eat a bean. (Blow on it first, ya big baby.) If it's crispy, you're done. If it's not, give it some more time.

SNACK ON LEGUMES, NOT NUTS

People who snack on nuts instead of potato chips deserve a pat on the back. Sure, they're a healthy choice. Go you! But too many nuts are a calorie bomb. If you're the kind of person who can eat 17 nuts, good for you. If you shovel them in by the handful, not so much.

Let's compare stats per cup:

Almonds: 823 calories, 71 g fat, 31 g carbs, 30 g protein
Cashews: 786 calories, 63 g fat, 45 g carbs, 21 g protein

Fava beans: 187 calories, 1 g fat, 33 g carbs, 13 g protein
Chickpeas: 269 calories, 4 g fat, 45 g carbs, 15 g protein
Green peas: 118 calories, 0.6 g fat, 21 g carbs, 8 g protein

BI BIM BAP-A-LULA

Bibimbap is just a Korean name for rice and a bunch of leftovers thrown together with a fried egg on top. Got leftover rice from takeout? Want some lunch? Have five minutes to spare? Bop, cat, bop. That's a Gene Vincent reference for you—he's famous for singing "Be-Bop-A-Lula" and "Blue Jean Bop," and was the first person inducted into the Rockabilly Hall of Fame. He'd have been even more famous if he was half as good-looking as Elvis Presley, but he wasn't. So here's your Korean bowl instead, Gene.

---

1. Coat a large frying pan with the oil and place over high heat.

2. Add the vegetables and kimchi. Partially cook for 3 minutes.

3. Add the rice with the soy sauce and stir-fry, mixing everything together.

4. Using a wooden spoon, press the rice mixture down and crisp the bottom of the rice. Leave it alone for a few minutes and listen to it sizzle.

5. Divide the rice between 2 plates.

6. Fry 2 eggs in the frying pan and top each plate with an egg. Hit it with some ground black pepper.

1 tablespoon canola oil

Whatever vegetables you have in your fridge that are at the end of their shelf life. (Here, I used red cabbage and an Indian green pea dish that was hanging around for a few days.)

½ cup Kip's Bay Refrigerator Kimchi (see page 160)

1 day-old container of takeout rice

1 tablespoon soy sauce

2 fried eggs

CHEAP-AND-EASY CHANA SAAG

I love Indian takeout—there's a wide variety of delicious and spicy food with almost unlimited vegetarian options. I could eat it every day (if I didn't mind dropping $40 plus on dinner for two, which I do). It has a great reputation as a healthy restaurant option, but after a few samosas, paratha bread, rice, and a couple of shared entrees, it's nearly as indulgent as anything else. That's because Indian joints fill their dishes with ghee, a form of clarified butter, cream, and a boatload of salt. Try this lightened-up version instead.

1 medium onion, chopped

2 garlic cloves

One 1-inch piece fresh ginger, peeled and chopped

6 cups fresh spinach

3 cups tomato puree

2 tablespoons curry powder

½ teaspoon garam masala

1 tablespoon hot paprika

1 teaspoon ground cumin

Pinch of kosher salt

1 cup water

Juice of 1 lemon

2 tablespoons coconut oil

4 cups chickpeas

2 cups sweet peas

1. Make your spice blend. Put the onion, garlic, ginger, 4 cups of the spinach, the tomato puree, curry, garam masala, paprika, cumin, salt, water, and lemon juice into a blender or food processor and blend it all together until you have an ugly, thick, green liquid.

2. Melt the coconut oil in a large pot over medium-low heat. Pour the spice blend in and simmer, uncovered, for 10 minutes.

3. Add the chickpeas, sweet peas, and the remaining 2 cups of spinach and stir to combine. Cover and simmer for 20 minutes.

4. Serve with quinoa or rice.

CURRIED CASHEWS WITH SPICY RED CABBAGE

*Vegan

Cashews and curry are like Voltron: when they combine, they make something exponentially greater than their individual parts. Instead of always doing the predictable thing and making a bean or pea curry, try one with nuts instead—but make sure you roast them first. Trust me, it's no big deal—the whole thing takes less than 30 minutes.

---

1. Preheat the oven to 350°F. Line a baking sheet with parchment paper.

2. Combine the curry, garam masala, paprika, and 1 tablespoon olive oil in a small bowl. Using a fork, mix until it becomes a paste.

3. Add the cashews and stir until they're covered evenly.

4. Place the cashews on the lined baking sheet. Sprinkle with salt and roast in the oven for 10 minutes.

5. Meanwhile, heat a glug of olive oil in a sauté pan over medium heat. Add the cabbage, cumin, turmeric, and a punch of salt and stir to combine. Stir-fry for 2 minutes. Reduce the heat to low, cover the pan, and let it cook until tender with a bit of crisp. (This should coincide with the cashew-roasting time.)

6. Serve the cabbage over quinoa with the cashews on top.

1 teaspoon curry powder

1 teaspoon garam masala

½ teaspoon hot paprika (cayenne or any other hot pepper works here, too)

Olive oil

1 cup cashews

1 head red cabbage, quartered and thinly sliced or shredded

1 tablespoon ground cumin

1 teaspoon ground turmeric

Kosher salt

Cooked quinoa (page 136) for serving

SHEPHERD'S PIE

Cybil Shepherd, Dax Shepard, Shepard Smith from Fox News, and Abraham (that one famous shepherd in the Bible) wouldn't agree on most things. I'm guessing here; I don't know any of them personally. But I'm confident that my Vegan Shepherd's Pie is better than any meat-and-cheese version they've ever had.

2 tablespoons olive oil

1 large onion, diced

1 pound carrots, peeled and chopped

1 bunch celery hearts, chopped

Kosher salt and ground black pepper

One 12-ounce package veggie ground beef substitute (Morningstar Farms Grillers Crumbles is my favorite.)

2 cups peas

1 teaspoon smoked paprika

2 tablespoons vegan gravy mix (I like Bistro or Gravy Master.)

10 ounces sliced mushrooms

1 tablespoon tomato paste

¾ cup water

4 potatoes (I like Yukon Gold with the skins on for this.)

½ bulb roasted garlic

1 tablespoon olive oil

½ cup unsweetened almond milk

3 slices Daiya nondairy cheese, roughly torn

1. Coat the bottom of a large pot with olive oil and place over medium heat. Add the onion and cook for 5 minutes.

2. Add the carrots and celery with a pinch of salt and pepper and cook for 5 minutes more.

3. Add the crumble, peas, paprika, gravy, mushrooms, tomato paste, and water, and stir to combine. Taste and adjust the seasoning. Cover the pot and simmer over medium-low heat for 5 minutes.

4. Preheat the oven to 350°F.

5. In a medium pot, cover the potatoes with cold water and bring to a boil. Boil the potatoes for 25 minutes while the stew cooks.

6. Drain and mash the potatoes. Add the softened garlic, olive oil, almond milk, Daiya, and lots of salt and pepper and stir them into the mash.

7. Spoon the stew mixture into a baking dish. Cover with a layer of the mashed potatoes. Use a fork to smooth out the potatoes.

8. Bake the pie in the preheated oven for 30 minutes. Let sit for 15 minutes, then slice and serve.

MANGU AND HUEVOS RANCHEROS MASH-UP

Huevos rancheros is a brunch staple, but I always want them to be better. To be honest, Mexican food in New York kind of sucks compared to LA or San Diego. But we have the best Dominican food in the country, hands down, including my favorite breakfast, mangu—mashed unripe plantains with fried onions. I married the two by swapping out tortillas for sweet plantains, which gives the black beans, onions, and slightly runny eggs a hint of sweetness.

1. Bring a big pot of water to a boil. Drop the plantains in and cook for 20 minutes.

2. Meanwhile, coat the bottom of a sauté pan with olive oil, add the onion, and stir to coat with the oil. Season the onions with a few shakes of adobo, stir, and cook over medium heat until slightly browned and fragrant.

3. Heat the beans and sofrito in a separate small pan. In another pan, cook your eggs over-easy or over-medium. (Actually, I don't care. Make your eggs however you want. It'll be great.)

4. Drain the plantains, reserving the cooking water, and transfer to a mixing bowl. Mash the plantains with a potato masher or a fork, add the butter, a shake of adobo, and some of the cooking water (as needed) and stir to combine. They should be mashed potato-like in texture.

5. Place a portion of the plantain mash on the bottom of a plate, top that with some beans, top that with onions, top that with an egg, then hit it with some hot sauce.

3 ripe plantains (think yellow with black leopard spots), peeled

Olive oil

1 large onion, sliced

Adobo seasoning

2 cups black beans, rinsed and drained

1 tablespoon sofrito

4 large eggs

1 tablespoon unsalted butter

½ cup reserved plantain cooking water

Hot sauce

TEMPEH BOLOGNESE

This is one of the few times I'll actually make a veggie version of a classic meat dish, because a life without Bolognese is no life at all. This is a great go-to dish because everyone likes it, there are a thousand different ways to make the sauce, and it's almost impossible to screw up. You can put it on spaghetti, on crostini, on polenta, poach some eggs in it, or eat it out of the pot with a spoon like an animal.

Olive oil

1 large onion, diced

Kosher salt and ground black pepper

4 garlic cloves, minced

8 ounces tempeh, grated

One 12-ounce jar roasted red peppers

One 14-ounce can tomatoes (plum or any kind you like)

1 tablespoon dried thyme

1 tablespoon dried basil

1 cup sweet peas

¼ cup red wine (one you'd actually drink)

¼ cup water

½ cup grated pecorino Romano cheese

1 tablespoon tomato paste

1. Cover the bottom of a pan with olive oil and place over medium heat. Add the onion and stir until coated with oil. Add a punch of salt and pepper and cook for 5 minutes until soft and translucent.

2. Stir in the garlic and tempeh and cook for another 3 minutes.

3. Meanwhile, puree the roasted peppers and tomatoes together in a blender or food processor.

4. Add the puree to the onion and garlic and stir to combine.

5. Add everything else to the pot and mix it up. Lower the heat a little and simmer, uncovered, for about 15 minutes, or until you have a chunky sauce. Taste and adjust the seasoning if needed.

PROTEIN SMOOTHIES

The hardest part of making a smoothie is washing the blender afterwards, which is way, way easier than cleaning a juicer. Any modern blender now separates into two parts and pops right into the dishwasher. I'm just saying, you can't use that as an excuse. Smoothies get people's eyes rolling because some people carry them as an accessory and food bloggers can't get enough of taking pictures of theirs like they just built the Taj Mahal. Don't make a big thing about it—just drink it.

A smoothie is the easiest way to load up on vitamin-rich vegetables, protein, fruit, and fiber, and it tastes like a milk shake. If you're having protein anxiety, a scoop of protein powder provides a quick 20 grams. They're a one-minute breakfast, a mid-day pick-me-up, or a post-workout recovery shake. Here are a few of my favorites.

ONE-MINUTE BREAKFAST SMOOTHIE

*Vegan

Throw all the ingredients in a blender and press the button until it's the consistency of a shake.

1 cup nut milk or water

1 heaping tablespoon peanut butter

1 banana, peeled and sliced

1 Bartlett pear, cored and sliced

2 cups spinach or whatever greens you have (Not lettuce, stupid.)

CRANBERRY-BANANA-APPLE PROTEIN SMOOTHIE

1 cup frozen cranberries

2 ripe (or slightly overripe) bananas, peeled and sliced

2 green apples, cored and sliced

1 teaspoon hemp seeds

1 teaspoon chia seeds

1 teaspoon almond butter

2 pitted dates

2 cups water

Throw all the ingredients in a blender and press the button until it's the consistency of a shake. Have you learned nothing from the last two recipes?

ONCE-YOU-GO-BLACKBERRY VEGAN POST-WORKOUT PROTEIN SHAKE

*Vegan

2 cups blackberries

3 apples, chopped

2 bananas, sliced

2 cups baby kale (or spinach)

2 cups cold water

2 scoops vegan protein powder
(Vega or Sunwarrior are best.)

Throw all the ingredients in a blender and press the button until it's the consistency of a shake.

3

I AIN'T AFRAID OF NO CARBS

Maybe it was Dr. Atkins, a yoga teacher, someone in your CrossFit box, or some other jerk trying to sell you something; but somebody scared you into thinking that sugar—what carbohydrates break down into during digestion—is poison. Unless you're some kind of fitness model on the day of a photo shoot (you're not and it isn't*), you have no reason to fall victim to "carb-o-phobia."

Let's be honest. Somehow, everyone in the world except Americans manage to eat rice, bread, pasta, and grains as a staple of their diet without becoming morbidly obese. French people really do carry unwieldy baguettes home for dinner in tote bags, Italians really do eat more pasta than any other country—by a lot, and the entire continent of Asia is fueled on refined white rice. They're not pretending to be cavemen, enduring juice cleanses, and whining about the headaches, lethargy, and foggy thinking that come with zero-carb diets.

Their secret is portion control. In other countries, life isn't a never-ending Olive Garden bread basket and all-you-can-shovel-in pasta bowl. Remember, the portion sizes you get in a restaurant can be four times larger than what you'd eat at home. So, let's all detox from this ridiculous line of thinking together and fall back in (moderate) love with carbs.

*If you're in the 0.0000001% of people who have been a cover model, sorry, and good for you. You look great.

PASTA: IN MY NEIGHBORHOOD, THEY CALL IT "MACARONI"

The Italians and the Japanese eat more pasta than anyone else in the world, and apart from that time they were on the wrong side of World War II, when have they been wrong about anything? On a scale of one to the best thing ever, the noodle-shop ramen in Tokyo and *cacio e pepe* in Rome is somewhere between having a threesome and winning the lotto. Maid cafes and tentacle porn? Sure, why not. The Coliseum? Yeah, OK. But those pasta bowls were life-changing experiences, the kind of shit you remember on your deathbed. So I'm here to take you to church and spread the macaroni gospel.

PEANUT BUTTER RAMEN

Peanut butter and jelly is a fine lunch, if you're eight years old. Grown-ass adults need to know about peanut butter and ramen. If you make this, it's the only thing you'll ever want to eat again—creamy peanut butter, ramen noodles, sesame oil, Sriracha, and some kale and mushrooms thrown in, because minerals, man. Pair it with a Sapporo and consider it a rite of passage.

1. Add oil to the bottom of a medium pot and place over medium heat. Throw the garlic in, and let cook for a minute. Toss in the scallions, kale, and mushrooms. Sprinkle on some salt and stir it around. Cover and let cook and soften for 5 to 7 minutes, then take it off the heat.

2. Bring a big pot of salty water to a boil. Add the ramen and cook for 3 minutes. Reserve $1/3$ cup of the cooking water for the next step.

3. Drain the noodles and put them back in the warm pot. Add the peanut butter, sesame oil, reserved ramen water, and Sriracha to the noodles. Stir to combine and coat the noodles evenly. Then add the vegetables and stir them in, too.

4. Divide the noodles among four bowls. Garnish with peanuts, nori, and sesame seeds.

3 garlic cloves, minced

1 bunch scallions, sliced (Cut the hairy root end off and use the whole scallion—green and white like the NY Jets)

1 cup kale, tough ribs removed

8 ounces mushrooms (any kind), sliced

3 packages instant ramen (but throw out the gross flavor packets)

3 tablespoons smooth peanut butter

2 tablespoons sesame oil (The darker the sesame oil, the better.)

$1/3$ cup ramen cooking water

2 tablespoons Sriracha (Use less if you're a hot food wuss.)

Peanuts

Nori

Sesame seeds

MISO-TAHINI RAMEN

*Vegan

This soup is all about the broth—think of the black sesame miso concoction as a pasta sauce that's so good you're going to want to drink it. And you should. Black sesame is crack sesame. The first time I tasted it in a Harajuku hole-in-the-wall ramen joint where you order from a vending machine, I knew I was hooked. This one's on me—try it *just this once*.

32 ounces vegetable broth

1 tablespoon white miso paste

1 tablespoon tahini

½ cup black sesame seeds

1 tablespoon Sriracha (or any chili sauce)

2 tablespoons tamari (or substitute soy sauce)

4 ounces dried tofu, diced

1 bunch scallions, white part only, chopped

12 ounces ramen noodles (fresh or dried, but throw out the flavor packet first)

1 head bok choy, greens only, chopped

2 tablespoons sesame oil

2 sheets nori

1. In a large pot over medium heat, whisk together the broth, miso, tahini, half of the sesame seeds, the Sriracha, tamari, tofu, and scallions until fully incorporated. Cover, and lower the heat a little. Cook for 15 minutes to develop flavor.

2. Bring a pot of salty water (ocean-water-level salty) to a boil.

3. Throw in your ramen noodles and cook: 2 minutes for fresh noodles, 5 minutes for dried.

4. Remove the noodles, but save the water.

5. Divide the noodles in half, and place each half in a separate big bowl.

6. Add the bok choy to the broth and carefully pour it over the noodles. Top off the bowl with some of the leftover ramen cooking water.

7. Garnish with sesame oil, sesame seeds, and nori.

8. Slurp it up. (The Japanese consider it a compliment to slurp, and so do I.)

SICHUAN-STYLE VEGGIE RAMEN

We tend to think of ramen as something distinctly Japanese, but until the 1940s, ramen in Japan was just called Chinese Noodle Soup. Some of the best ramen I tasted in Yokohama was in Chinese noodle houses. It was completely different, with a slightly lighter broth and a potent dose of Sichuan heat. The heat also clears your sinuses for the ultimate sick food. Fuck chicken soup.

---

1. In a large soup pot, combine everything except for the noodles, sesame seeds, bean sprouts, and sesame oil. Stir to blend the flavors and bring to a boil. Reduce to a low simmer, cover, and let cook for 20 minutes. It'll get spicier and more delicious as it cooks.

2. Bring another pot of water to a boil and cook the noodles: 2 minutes for fresh noodles, 5 minutes for dried.

3. Remove the noodles, but reserve the cooking water.

4. Divide the noodles evenly among four big bowls—or 2 huge bowls if you want to do it up fat-bastard style.

5. Ladle the soup and vegetables over the noodles. Add the reserved ramen cooking water if you want a soupier texture.

6. Garnish with sesame seeds, bean sprouts, sesame oil, and maybe a little chili sauce.

4 garlic cloves, minced

1 leek, thinly sliced (Clean it well.)

1 bunch fresh chives, chopped

8 ounces seitan, cubed

2 cups baby corn

1 cup spinach leaves

1 quart vegetable broth

1 quart water

1 to 3 tablespoons Sichuan chili sauce (Start with 1 tablespoon if you're not a capsaicin junkie—you can always add more.)

1 tablespoon ground ginger

1 tablespoon shoyu (or soy sauce)

4 ounces ramen noodles, fresh or dried

Sesame seeds

Bean sprouts

A shake of dark sesame oil

Sriracha or other chili sauce (optional)

SOY SAUCE SOBA

Soba. It's ramen's less-sexy cousin. If the McCarthy family were Japanese noodles, ramen would be the hot blonde immunologist/ former playmate (Jenny), and Soba would be her thicker, more substantial cousin/ Ghostbuster (Melissa). Soba noodles are made from buckwheat, a more nutritious grain than the white flour used to make ramen, and the flavor is more defined.

1. In a medium pot, combine the water, soy sauce, ginger, miso, mirin, Sriracha, and mushrooms. Stir, cover, and let simmer for 20 minutes.

2. Bring a small pot of water to a boil. Carefully place the eggs (still in their shells) in the water. Boil for 1 minute. Turn off the heat and let the eggs sit in the water, covered, for 10 minutes. Using a slotted spoon, remove the eggs, and transfer to a bowl filled with cold water.

3. Fill a medium pot with salty water and bring to a boil. Add the noodles and cook until al dente, 3 to 5 minutes.

4. Meanwhile, peel the eggs and slice each egg in half lengthwise.

5. Drain the noodles. Hit them with a little sesame oil to avoid clumping. Divide evenly among four bowls.

6. Cover the noodles with the soy sauce broth and drop in an egg.

7. Garnish with nori, inari age, and sesame seeds.

6 cups water

½ cup soy sauce

½ teaspoon ground ginger

1 tablespoon white miso paste

2 tablespoons mirin

1 tablespoon Sriracha or any chili sauce

3 ounces shiitake mushrooms, stemmed and sliced

4 large eggs

8 ounces soba noodles

Sesame oil

1 sheet nori

2 ounces inari age (That's that tofu skin you see at sushi joints. If you don't have access to it, use thinly sliced tofu.)

½ teaspoon sesame seeds

DON'T BOTHER MAKING YOUR OWN PASTA

Please don't be the person who thinks it's cool and "authentic" to make your own homemade pasta. Unless you're doing it for a living, or have a lot of experience making pasta, it's going to suck—it'll be floppy, too hard in some places and too soft in others, and likely to turn into one mushy blob. You think people in Italy are making their own pasta like it's 1890? Nope. Unless it's gnocchi (or some weird Northern Italian dish you've likely never heard of), it's coming out of a box.

30-MINUTE MARINARA

*Vegan

Put down the jar of sauce. What are you, some kind of animal? Making pasta sauce is no big deal. Life is not the movies—when Italian women make tomato sauce, they don't spend all day in black widow drag, stirring a cauldron like a witch. In Italy, pasta is lightly dressed in sauce, not drowning in it the way it's served in the U.S. Got a half hour? Then you can make a traditional marinara. Remember, Grandma doesn't have all day for this shit. She has to watch her stories.

1. Pour a glug of olive oil into a large sauté pan. Swish it around and place the pan over medium heat. Add the carrots and sauté for 5 minutes.

2. Add the garlic and a pinch of salt. Cook until the garlic sizzles and becomes fragrant. (Don't burn it.)

3. Mash the tomatoes with a potato masher or crush them with your (clean) hand, then add to the skillet. Pour the juices from the tomato can in, and add a cup of broth or water. Stir in the red pepper flakes, bay leaf, oregano, thyme, and black pepper.

4. Simmer for 15 minutes or until your sauce thickens. Taste and adjust the seasoning, then simmer for 10 minutes more. Stir in the sugar. (Take out the damn bay leaf.)

5. Drop some fresh, torn basil leaves on top, and your sauce is done.

6. Bring a large pot of salty water to a boil. Add the bucatini and cook for 2 minutes less than the instructions on the box tell you.

7. Drain the pasta and finish cooking for the last 2 minutes in the marinara sauce.

JUST THE TIP: Melt ¼ cup of gorgonzola cheese into the marinara for an incredible creamy, strong cheesy sauce.

Glug of olive oil

1 carrot, peeled and cut into small dice (about ½ cup)

5 garlic cloves, minced or thinly sliced (who cares what you do?)

One 28-ounce can San Marzano tomatoes

1 cup vegetable broth (or water)

A fistful of salt

Pinch of crushed red pepper flakes

1 bay leaf

½ teaspoon dried oregano

½ teaspoon dried thyme

¼ teaspoon ground black pepper

½ teaspoon sugar

Torn fresh basil leaves

1 pound of bucatini (It's like spaghetti, but thicker, with a hollow hole in the center of the noodle).

SPAGHETTI WITH GREEK DILL PESTO

Without Greece, the world wouldn't have democracy, grouchy diner owners, feta cheese, George Michael (RIP) and Criss Angel (born Georgios Kyriacos Panayiotou and Christopher Nicholas Sarantakos, respectively), and Arianna Huffington. Just try to imagine a world without HuffPo and their awesome paying-writers-with-exposure-not-money policy. That's not civilization, which the Greeks will also tell you they invented.

1. Make the pesto: Place all the ingredients into a food processor and blend until you have a thick, saucy texture. Dip your (clean) pinkie in, and taste. Adjust the seasoning if needed.

2. Cook the spaghetti: Bring a big pot of salty water to a boil. Throw in the pasta and boil for 8 minutes. Drain and set aside.

3. Coat the bottom of the same pot with olive oil and place over medium heat.

4. Return the spaghetti to the pot. Cover with the pesto; add the nuts, olives, feta, and black pepper. Stir over medium heat for 2 minutes.

5. Eat hot, cold, or at room temperature. Serve with a platter of fresh tomatoes and cucumbers slathered in olive oil, some good bread, and a couple of bottles of Greek white wine.

FOR THE DILL PESTO

1 bunch fresh dill

2 garlic cloves

½ cup feta cheese

Juice of 1 lemon

2 teaspoons dried oregano (1 tablespoon if you're the kind of big shot that uses fresh oregano)

¼ cup olive oil

¼ cup water

Kosher salt and ground black pepper

FOR THE SPAGHETTI

8 ounces dry spaghetti

Olive oil

Dill Pesto (see above)

¼ cup pine nuts, toasted in the oven at 350°F for 10 minutes, or in a dry pan over medium heat

¼ cup sliced Kalamata olives

½ cup crumbled feta cheese

Ground black pepper

THAI MACARONI SALAD

The only people who get excited about macaroni salad are Hawaiians, and they think Spam is food. Look, it's elbow noodles slathered in mayo. Then, for a thrill, people bring it outside for a BBQ and place it next to the potato salad (which is same thing with potatoes instead of pasta—real inventive). It bakes in the sun as the mayo slowly turns, sending guests running to the bathroom like they binged on Taco Bell. Instead, try a light and sweet, spicy and aromatic Thai-inspired macaroni salad with some texture and complexity. Bonus: no food poisoning.

10 ounces vermicelli noodles

6 scallions, thinly sliced

1 carrot, peeled and grated

1 seedless cucumber, thinly sliced

2 mangoes, cut into medium dice

1 cup peanuts

1 bunch fresh basil, leaves roughly torn

2 cups bean sprouts

Finely grated zest of 1 lime

Juice of 3 limes

¼ cup olive oil

¼ cup sesame oil

1 tablespoon maple syrup

2 tablespoons Sriracha (or whatever chili sauce you like)

1 tablespoon soy sauce

1 tablespoon creamy peanut butter

Black sesame seeds

1. Bring a pot of salty water to a boil. Add the noodles and cook for 3 minutes.

2. Drain in a strainer. Run cold water over the noodles until cold.

3. Transfer the noodles to a large bowl. Add the scallions, carrot, cucumber, mangoes, peanuts, basil, and bean sprouts.

4. In a large bowl, whisk together the lime zest, lime juice, oils, maple syrup, Sriracha, soy sauce, and peanut butter until you have a dressing.

5. Pour the dressing into a jar with a cover and shake.

6. Pour half of the dressing over the salad. Toss to combine. Cover and refrigerate the remaining dressing for another use.

7. Plate the salad in bowls, garnish with sesame seeds, then eat with chopsticks like that's your thing.

PENNE TIKKA MASALA WITH PEAS AND CASHEWS

What if you're craving Indian and Italian food at the same time? If you can't choose between the two, don't. This is obscenely good, and really easy to pull off. Make it when people come over and impress your friends and family who claim they don't like Indian food.

2 tablespoons butter

1 large onion, thinly sliced

5 garlic cloves, thinly sliced

1 teaspoon ground ginger

Kosher salt

1 tablespoon tomato paste

1 teaspoon hot paprika

1 tablespoon smoked paprika

3 tablespoons honey

¼ teaspoon crushed red pepper flakes

1 tablespoon garam masala

One 28-ounce can tomatoes, pureed

One 10-ounce package frozen green peas, defrosted

1 cup heavy cream

1 cup water

1 cup cashews

1 pound penne pasta

1 bunch fresh cilantro for garnish

1. Melt the butter in a large saucepan. Add the onion, garlic, ginger, and salt and stir to coat. Sauté on medium heat for 5 minutes until the onions are soft. (Don't burn the damn garlic.)

2. Add the tomato paste, both kinds of paprika, honey, garam masala, and red pepper flakes. Stir into the onion mix. If your kitchen doesn't smell amazing, you're doing something wrong.

3. Add the tomato puree, peas, cream, and water. Get it bubbling on a high simmer and cook, uncovered, for about 20 minutes or until thickened into a thick gravy. Taste and adjust the spice and salt levels if needed. Stir in the cashews.

4. Meanwhile, cook and drain the pasta. Dress the pasta with the tikka masala sauce, and garnish with cilantro.

ISRAELI COUSCOUS WITH RED CHARD AND SLOW-POACHED EGG

I've seen a million recipes for poached eggs, and I've found a million ways to fuck them up. I've stirred the water and made a tiny whirlpool vortex. I've added white vinegar. I've made cute little Saran-wrapped egg packages. I somehow always end up with a raw salmonella bomb, or an overcooked rock. Luckily, David Chang is even more obsessed with the perfect poached egg than I am, and his quasi-Japanese slow-poach method is the best (and easiest). I've taken it a step further and simplified it so even you can do it. No thermometers needed. You can't screw it up even if it's your intention to make a sub-par poached egg. This is "unfuckupable."

1. Place a steamer basket in the bottom of a large pot. Put the eggs in the basket, and fill the pot three-quarters of the way with very hot tap water. Place over one of the small burners on your stovetop and bring the water to a boil. Adjust the heat to the lowest setting and let cook for 20 minutes. Then turn the heat off and let the eggs have a steam bath for 25 minutes.

2. Meanwhile, melt the butter in a medium saucepan over medium-high heat. Add the onion, garlic, and a punch of salt. Stir well and turn the heat up a little higher.

3. Remove the stems from the chard and slice them into small pieces. Add to the onion mixture and stir. Chop the rest of the chard and add to the mix. The onions should be fragrant and brown-ish. If they aren't, wait until they are, then add the couscous. Stir and cook for 1 minute.

4. Add the broth, cover, and bring to a boil. Reduce to the lowest heat and cook for 10 minutes. Turn off the heat and let sit for 5 minutes. Taste and adjust the seasoning if needed.

5. Divide the couscous among four bowls or plates.

6. Crack the eggs, one at a time, into a small cup. Then slide the egg from the cup on top of the couscous. Crack some black pepper on the egg.

7. Eat it. But first, break the egg apart and let the yolk dribble out to make the perfect sauce.

4 large eggs, at room temperature
(or at least not freezing)

2 tablespoons butter

1 large onion, thinly sliced

4 garlic cloves, grated on a
microplane

Kosher salt and freshly cracked
black pepper

1 bunch red chard

1 cup Israeli couscous (the kind
that looks like little round pellets,
not grains of sand)

2 cups vegetable broth

LIFE-CHANGING BUTTERNUT MAC AND CHEESE

Why are all our great memories of the mac and cheese we ate as a kid ruined when we eat the weird, dry versions our friends and family make? It's because the secret was that weird chemical cheese powder or a generous squeeze of Velveeta. I have created my own creamy orange sauce to slather on your inner fat-kid favorite—but mine is made with real butternut squash, French herbs, white wine, and, ooh-la-la, a roux. Bring this to Thanksgiving, family BBQs, or just to someone's house to put their aunt's mac and cheese to shame.

---

1 bunch asparagus

1 pound gemelli pasta

½ cup plus 2 tablespoons butter

1 large onion

5 garlic cloves

1 cup fresh basil leaves

½ cup white wine

½ cup flour (Use all-purpose or whatever hippie flour you like.)

4 cups butternut squash soup (The kind that comes in a carton.)

2 tablespoons fresh thyme

1 tablespoon herbes de Provence

Kosher salt and ground black pepper

1 cup soft goat cheese

1 cup ricotta salata cheese (Smoked gouda is kind of awesome, too.)

1. Blanch the asparagus for 1 minute in salty boiling water. (Salty, like where seahorses live.) Remove, and run cold water over the asparagus to cool. Cut into small rounds.

2. Slightly undercook the pasta. If the instructions say 10 minutes, cook it for 8. You want Al dente with a bold, capital A. Drain in a colander, run some cold water over it, and set aside with the asparagus.

3. Melt 2 tablespoons of the butter to cover the bottom of a large saucepan.

4. In a food processor, combine the onion, garlic, and basil and pulse until it looks like salsa.

5. Add the onion, basil, and garlic mixture to the saucepan with a pinch of salt and the wine. Increase the heat to high and sauté until the wine evaporates. Remove from the pan and set aside.

6. Melt the remaining ½ cup butter over medium heat, add the flour, and stir to combine. Cook until it turns medium brown (a little more than 5 minutes).

7. Whisk in the butternut soup one cup at a time until you have a smooth sauce. Keep cooking and stirring until it thickens, about 10 minutes.

8. Turn off the heat and stir in the thyme and herbes de Provence. Taste and adjust the seasoning. Congratulations, you made a béchamel.

9. Preheat the oven to 400°F.

10. Add the pasta and asparagus to the butternut béchamel. Stir to combine with the heat on the lowest setting.

11. Stir in the goat cheese and ricotta salata until completely melted and incorporated.

12. In a small bowl, combine the pecorino Romano cheese, bread crumbs, and 1 tablespoon of olive oil. Stir to combine.

13. Pour the pasta into a baking dish. Top with the bread-crumb mixture. Bake for 15 minutes until the bread crumbs are golden brown.

14. Remove from the oven. Let sit for 10 minutes, hit it with some salt and freshly ground pepper, and serve.

¼ cup pecorino Romano cheese
½ cup panko bread crumbs
Olive oil

THREE-CHEESE ORZO

Who has the time and energy to make a real risotto? I don't care what the recipe tells you; risotto always takes 45 minutes, and all that stirring will leave your forearms sore for days. Let's simplify that. Imagine *cacio e pepe*, mac and cheese, and risotto getting together to form a delicious *ménage à trois* that doesn't end awkwardly. It looks like rice, so tell your friends it's risotto; they won't know the difference.

1½ cups orzo pasta

Glug of olive oil

2 garlic cloves, sliced

4 ounces fresh spinach

2 teaspoons freshly ground black pepper

2 tablespoons grated Parmigiano-Reggiano cheese, plus extra for serving

2 tablespoons grated pecorino Romano cheese, plus extra for serving

¼ cup mascarpone cheese

Truffle salt (optional, but you really should)

Kosher salt

1. Bring a pot of salty water to a boil. Add the orzo and cook for 8 minutes. Drain.

2. Cover the bottom of a large sauté pan with olive oil and place over medium heat. Add the garlic and cook for 2 minutes. Add the spinach with a pinch of salt. Stir and cook until wilted, about 1 minute.

3. Remove the pan from the heat, add the pasta to the pan, and stir in the cheeses until melted and well combined. Hit it hard with freshly ground black pepper. Taste and adjust the seasoning (add truffle salt now if using).

4. Serve family-style in a large bowl with some grated cheese on top.

GNOCCHI WITH GORGONZOLA, WALNUTS, AND ARUGULA

In my never-ending quest to completely gentrify mac and cheese, I bring you this version that takes less time to make than the one in the box.

Let's talk about gnocchi for a second, shall we? Unless you look like Sophia Petrillo or make your own gnocchi on the regular, just buy the $2 vacuum pack at the supermarket. Your version sucks. Your family and friends are just being nice when they compliment you on your soft mush "gah-bidge" gnocchi.

---

1. Get a pot of salty water boiling.

2. Meanwhile, in a pan over medium heat, toast the walnuts.

3. Boil the gnocchi for 3 minutes until they all float to the top of the water. Reserve ½ cup of the cooking water. Drain the gnocchi.

4. Put the cheese and water in what used to be the gnocchi pot. Set that over medium heat. Give it a stir until it melts. Add the gnocchi, walnuts, salt, and pepper. Stir to coat, and taste for seasoning. Throw in the arugula and mix it up.

5. How easy was that?

1 cup walnut halves

One 1-pound package gnocchi

½ cup reserved cooking water

1 cup gorgonzola cheese

Punch of salt (If you have truffle salt, now's the time.)

Lots and lots of ground black pepper

1 cup arugula (or a head of radicchio)

BLUE CHEESE, PEAR, AND PECAN MAC AND CHEESE

There's a lot more to blue cheese than buffalo wing dipping sauce. So what if it smells like old gym shoes? Use blue cheese for your mac and cheese and it'll taste posh. This is a riff on the classic Italian combo of gorgonzola, walnuts, pears, pancetta, and pasta. That's a good thing, but not the only thing. Try it my way.

12 ounces rotini pasta (Any pasta will work.)

Olive oil

1 shallot, diced

5 ounces Lightlife Organic Fakin' Bacon Tempeh Strips (so will any vegetarian bacon), diced

3 pears, peeled, cored, and cut into slices (Use firm pears here, you don't want mush.)

1 head radicchio, sliced

6 ounces blue cheese, crumbled

1½ cups reserved cooking water (or sub in milk for a creamier sauce)

Kosher salt and freshly ground black pepper if you have it. If not the regular kind is fine, too

4 ounces pecan halves, toasted in the oven at 350°F for 10 minutes

1. Fill a pot with salty water and bring it to a boil. Add the pasta and slightly undercook (2 minutes less than the box instructions). Reserve 2 cups of the cooking water. Drain the pasta and leave it in the colander.

2. Using the same pot (you don't have to use every pot in the house), coat the bottom with a little olive oil and place over medium heat. Add the shallot and a pinch of salt and sauté for 3 minutes. Add the veggie bacon and cook for 5 minutes more, stirring frequently.

3. Add the pears and radicchio and season with a little salt and pepper. Stir and cook for 3 minutes.

4. Add the blue cheese and ½ cup of the reserved cooking water. Lower the heat, and stir until it melts down into a sauce that coats the back of the spoon. If you have to add more water here, do it; that's why we reserved 2 cups.

5. Add the undercooked pasta, and finish cooking it in the sauce. Taste and season with salt and lots of pepper.

6. Serve topped with the toasted pecans.

HERBED ORZO WITH FETA AND FIGS

This light version of mac and cheese tastes like a Greek summer. Mint, basil, lemon, feta, oregano, toasted nuts, and figs combine to make this a fresh and unexpected take on a barbecue classic. Any other mac and cheese at the party will be going home in Tupperware if you bring this. The ingredients aren't cheap for this: Greek always costs extra.

1 cup pecan halves

1 pound orzo pasta

1 bunch fresh basil, washed and leaves picked

1 bunch fresh mint, washed and leaves picked

6 ounces feta cheese, crumbled

5 ounces Kalamata olives, pitted and chopped

8 ounces dried figs, stemmed and quartered

Juice of 2 lemons

1 teaspoon balsamic vinegar

1 teaspoon honey

2 tablespoons olive oil

1 teaspoon dried oregano

Kosher salt and ground black pepper

1. Preheat the oven to 350°F. Spread out the pecans on a sheet pan and toast for 10 minutes. Set aside.

2. Meanwhile, get a really big pot of salty water boiling. Throw the orzo in and cook for 7 minutes. Drain and transfer to a bowl.

3. Add the basil, mint, feta, olives, and figs to the hot orzo and stir well.

4. In a small jar, combine the lemon juice, vinegar, honey, olive oil, and oregano. Shake it up, and pour it over the orzo mixture. Season with salt and pepper and stir it up. Taste and adjust the seasoning as needed.

5. Eat this hot, cold, or at room temperature.

UDON NOODLES WITH CREAMY VEGAN RAMP AND DANDELION PESTO

Vegan

I recently ate a gross Kale Udon Bowl at a Japanese restaurant. They made zero effort; just threw some garlic, kale, and noodles in a bowl and acted like that was acceptable. I'm not even vegan, but I was offended on behalf of vegans everywhere. I went to the greenmarket where they were all excited about ramps and fiddleheads and dandelions. I filled a bag and made it my mission to create the best vegan udon bowl ever. I succeeded.

1 bunch ramps, washed well, then washed again

1 bunch dandelion greens, stems trimmed, chopped

1 avocado, pitted and peeled

⅓ cup olive oil

⅓ cup nutritional yeast (or Parmesan cheese for nonvegans)

⅓ cup water

2 teaspoons sugar

1 teaspoon kosher salt (Gentile salt works, too.)

Juice of 1 lemon

1 cup cashews

⅓ cup raisins

Pinch of crushed red pepper flakes

1 pound dried udon noodles (Use fresh if you want. I don't care.)

1. Cut the greens off of the ramps. Separate the greens from the whites. Chop the greens. Mince the white part like garlic, and set aside.

2. Combine 1 cup of the dandelion greens, 1 cup of the ramp greens, the avocado flesh, olive oil, nutritional yeast, water, sugar, 1 teaspoon of the minced ramps, salt, and lemon in a blender or food processor, and pulse until it forms a pesto.

3. In a dry pan over medium heat, toast the cashews until fragrant.

4. Coat the bottom of a sauté pan with olive oil, and place over medium heat. Add the remaining minced ramps, ramp greens, dandelion greens, raisins, and red pepper flakes.

5. Bring a big pot of salty water to a boil, add the udon, and cook for 8 minutes. Drain the noodles and return to the pot. Add the pesto and toss to coat the pasta evenly. Toss the greens and ramps with the pasta. Add the toasted cashews and make it look pretty.

JUST THE TIP: Get to the farmers' market late in the day, around 5:00 or 6:00 p.m. Those small farmers get up mad early, and they want to GTFO of there. They'll be willing to do buy one/get one, or slash the prices to sell off their inventory and go home. Have a chat, make a deal; everybody leaves happy.

"ARAB" RICE

Isaac is my seventy-year-old Israeli buddy who lives downstairs. One day, in the lobby, he says, "You, Chef, what you eat today?" I told him I had leftover rice, so I made a cross between mujadara and Persian rice. His sour expression made it clear that he didn't have much confidence in me, but he took some home anyway. Two hours later, he's banging on my door, saying it's the best rice he's had in his life and now I have to teach his wife how to make it. He actually smiled and said my "Arab Rice" reminded him of his childhood, that it was like the food he grew up with—"but better." It was the single best reaction anyone has ever had to my cooking.

Olive oil

2 cups basmati rice

Punch (not a pinch) of kosher salt

4 cups vegetable broth

2 onions, cut into medium dice

½ pound mushrooms (whatever kind you have), chopped

½ cup almonds, roughly chopped

¼ cup raisins or dried cranberries

1 tablespoon ground cumin

½ teaspoon ground coriander

½ bunch of dill fronds, finely chopped

Kale chip(s) for garnish

1. Cover the bottom of a large saucepan with olive oil and place over medium heat.

2. Add the rice and salt and stir to coat the rice with the oil. When the rice begins to make a sizzling sound, add the broth and bring to a boil.

3. Reduce the heat to the lowest point, cover the pot, and simmer for 20 minutes.

4. Keep the rice covered and remove from the heat.

5. Meanwhile, warm some olive oil in a large sauté pan over medium-high heat. Add the onions and salt and stir to combine. Cook until brown, stirring frequently, about 30 minutes. (I know it's a long time, but it's totally worth it. The key to unlocking the awesomeness of this dish is caramelizing the onions.)

6. Add the mushrooms, almonds, raisins, cumin, and coriander to the onions. Cook for about 5 minutes, until the mushrooms have browned and the mixture smells nutty.

7. Combine the rice and onion mixture in the saucepan. Make sure to scrape the sauté pan well to get all the brown bits in there.

8. Over low heat, stir in the dill until all the ingredients are well combined. Taste and adjust the seasoning if needed.

9. Top with a kale chip. People will think, farm-to-table.

KALE CHIPS ARE NO BIG DEAL

You can buy them in any supermarket or just tear up some kale leaves, coat with olive oil, hit them with salt and pepper, and bake in a 350°F oven until they turn from leaves into chips.

RICE CAKE BOWL

*Low-cal

This whole thing is less than 200 calories a serving, with the egg and avocado. Compare that with a 1000 plus calorie disaster of a rice bowl you'd get in a restaurant. I'm not saying mine tastes more decadent, but at least you won't look pregnant after eating it. (Unless you're already pregnant. Congratulations?)

1. In a small bowl, whisk together the miso, lemon, Sriracha, and sesame oil to make your sauce. Set aside.

2. Boil the rice cakes and the spinach together for 10 minutes in water. Toss in a punch of salt. Drain in a colander and return to the pot.

3. Over low heat, add the sauce, kimchi, scallions, and radishes to the rice cake–spinach mixture. Cook for a few minutes, but allow the vegetables to maintain their crunchiness. Taste and adjust the seasoning if needed.

4. Divide among four bowls, and top with sliced egg and avocado.

1 tablespoon white miso paste

Juice of 1 lemon

½ teaspoon Sriracha

1 teaspoon sesame oil

1 pound rice cakes

One 10-ounce package frozen spinach, thawed

Punch of kosher salt

1 cup Kip's Bay Refrigerator Kimchi (see page 160)

6 scallions, sliced

6 radishes, thinly sliced

4 hard-boiled eggs, sliced (Boil eggs for 3 minutes; let sit in the hot water covered for 10 minutes.)

1 avocado, pitted, peeled, and sliced

100-CALORIE ASIAN GNOCCHI

*Vegan   *Low-cal

I'm not selling snake oil here. One serving of this recipe is only 100 calories. (OK, 111 calories—the same as nine Pringles. I rounded down, so sue me.) This is all thanks to the magic of Samhak Mini Rice Cakes. They have a gnocchi-like look and feel, but they're made of rice. Buy them at your local Asian market or if you live someplace boring, order them online. That entire package of rice cakes is only 120 calories and there are just three ingredients: rice, water, and salt.

---

1. Fill a medium saucepan with water and bring to a boil.

2. Blanch the snow peas in the boiling water for 1 minute. Transfer to a colander and run cold water over them. Reserve the boiling water.

3. Add the rice cakes to the boiling water and cook for 10 minutes. Drain and set aside.

4. Meanwhile, in a small mixing bowl, whisk together the lime juice, sesame oil, tamari, Sriracha, and maple syrup until combined. There's your sauce.

5. Place a large skillet over medium-high heat and add the scallions and tofu, stirring frequently for a minute or two.

6. Add the rice cakes, snow peas, and sauce. Stir until combined and rice cakes are evenly coated with the sauce.

7. Portion it out for four, and top each serving with toasted sesame seeds if you feel like it.

4 ounces snow peas (Take a second to peel the stringy part off so you don't choke on it.)

1 pound Samhak Mini Rice Cakes

Juice of 1 lime

1 teaspoon sesame oil

1 tablespoon tamari

1 tablespoon Sriracha

1 teaspoon maple syrup

1 bunch scallions, sliced lengthwise into thin strips

2 ounces dried tofu

HOPPIN' HASSAN: HOPPIN JOHN'S COUSIN FROM LEBANON

*Vegan

To celebrate the new year, Southern Italians eat lentils for good luck. (On December 31st, my mother will actually call me to make sure I'm planning on eating lentil soup.) American Southerners eat Hoppin' John, a rice and beans dish for luck. I kinda sorta combined the two and made the ultimate rice and lentil dish: mujadara. You can eat it any day, but time it right for the luckiest year ever.

¾ cup olive oil (Not extra virgin—use the cheap, slutty kind.)

3 huge onions, thinly sliced

Punch (not a pinch) of kosher salt

1 tablespoon ground turmeric

2 cups lentils (black or green French Puy lentils; just not red, since they get mushy)

3 tablespoons ground cumin (It sounds like a lot, and it is. But trust me here.)

2 teaspoons smoked pepper (If you can, use Turkish Urfa biber pepper; ground black pepper works in a pinch.)

7 cups vegetable broth

2 cups basmati rice

4 cups water

Green olives

Pomegranate seeds

1. Pour the oil into your biggest soup pot. Get it hot and throw in the onions, salt, and turmeric. Stir to evenly coat the onions with oil. Keep the heat on medium. Fry the onions until they become chocolate-brown. The key to this is not stirring too much. Let them fry for 10 minutes, and then stir once to see where you are. Let them fry for another 10, and give 'em another stir. Ten minutes more, undisturbed, should get your onions where you want them.

2. Add the lentils, cumin, and pepper to the onions and fry for one more minute. Does your kitchen smell awesome yet?

3. Add the broth and bring to a boil. Reduce to a simmer, cover, and cook for about 45 minutes. You want your lentils tender, not mushy or rock hard.

4. In a medium pot, combine the rice and water and bring to a boil. Reduce to a simmer, cover, and cook for 20 minutes.

5. Add the rice to the pot of cooked lentils and stir. Taste and adjust the seasoning.

6. Stick some olives and pomegranate seeds on top to make it look nice, and serve.

ADDICTIVE COCONUT-SAFFRON RICE

`*Vegan`

I was a private chef for a couple who had a gallon-a-week coconut rice habit. They started calling it "Crack Rice" and requesting more and more . . . until all they wanted to do was veg out on their couch and gorge themselves on the yellow stuff. It's the easiest thing in the world to make. A recipe from a genius blog called Papawow inspired this dish, but the conspiracy theorist in me thinks the CIA really invented it to get people hooked.

1. In a medium bowl, soak the saffron in the 2 cups of water. Using a wooden spoon, break the saffron up and stir.

2. In a medium saucepan, toast the cumin seeds until fragrant.

3. Add 1 tablespoon of the coconut oil and the shallot to the pan and sauté over medium heat for 5 to 7 minutes until soft and translucent. Add the rice and bouillon, stir to coat, and cook for 2 minutes more.

4. Add the saffron water and the coconut milk and stir to combine. Cover the pot and bring to a boil. Reduce to a simmer and let cook for 15 minutes.

5. Remove from the heat and stir in the remaining 1 tablespoon of coconut oil.

6. Find the number of a reputable rehab facility.

A two-finger pinch of saffron. (I know, the stuff is expensive like printer ink, but it's an investment. If you're really broke, use turmeric, but don't come running to me when it's not the same.)

2 cups water

½ teaspoon cumin seeds

2 tablespoons coconut oil

1 shallot, cut into small dice

2 cups white basmati rice

2 tablespoons veggie soup base or 2 bouillon cubes

2 cups light coconut milk

BREAD

Here's the thing. If you have a fresh loaf of good bread, any recipe I give you is going to ruin it. Just eat the damn bread. Break off a hunk, eat it plain, butter it, spread some chocolate on it if you're feeling sophisticated. That's all you have to do, because it's fresh fucking bread.

Now, if you have some half-assed packaged bread from the supermarket or not-so-fresh bread, I can help.

GRILLED PEACH PANZANELLA

Panzanella is just a fancy way of saying "stale bread salad" in Italian. When my grandmother had a bunch of stale bread hanging around and we were already up to our ears in bread crumbs, she used that bread to make a panzanella. You probably think you're too good for stale bread and just toss it, or your spiritual guru says you're gluten intolerant, or you swore off carbs so your beach pics will look hot on Instagram. Let me change your mind.

---

1. Preheat a grill pan over medium-high heat.

2. Toss the peaches with the balsamic vinegar until coated. Place them flesh side down on the hot grill and cook for 3 minutes. Flip them over and cook for another 3 minutes. Set aside to cool.

3. In a large bowl, toss the peaches with the rest of the ingredients. Taste and adjust the seasoning.

4. Let it sit for 30 minutes so the flavors can get together, and then serve.

4 peaches, each sliced into eighths
1 tablespoon balsamic vinegar
½ loaf stale, toasted, or grilled Italian bread, cubed
1 shallot, minced
1 cup fresh basil, minced
1 bunch celery hearts, chopped
2 cups grape tomatoes, halved
½ cup crumbled feta (vegan or dairy)
1 tablespoon red wine vinegar
2 tablespoons olive oil
Kosher salt and ground black pepper

ARTICHOKE AND MUSHROOM STRATA

Has anyone in the history of the world bought a loaf of bread and eaten the whole thing before it got all stale and/or moldy? I'm constantly stuck with bread on life support, but luckily, we can turn that stale-ish bread into an awesome dinner. Enter strata. It's like an Italian version of bread pudding, but in this case we're not making it for dessert. Call it a casserole.

Glug of olive oil

1 onion, cut into medium dice

2 pinches of kosher salt

½ pound cremini mushrooms, stemmed and quartered

2 tablespoons minced garlic

1 tablespoon capers

1 tablespoon dried thyme

One 12-ounce can artichoke hearts, drained and chopped

6 large eggs

1 cup whole milk

1 cup grated Parmigiano-Reggiano cheese

4 cups bread (any kind), cubed

1 cup shredded Gruyère cheese

Black pepper

1. Heat the oil in a sauté pan over medium heat. Add the onion and salt and stir to combine. Let cook for 5 minutes, or until onion becomes translucent.

2. Add the mushrooms, garlic, capers, thyme, and artichokes. Stir and cook for 10 minutes. Set aside.

3. In a large bowl, whisk the eggs, milk, and Parmigiano-Reggiano together until combined. Add the bread, Gruyère, and mushroom mixture with another punch of salt and a healthy amount of black pepper and combine well; the bread should be soaked with the egg and cheese mixture.

4. Pour into a baking dish and cover with plastic wrap. Refrigerate for at least 4 hours.

5. Preheat the oven to 350°F.

6. Take the strata out of the fridge, remove the plastic wrap, and bake in the preheated oven for 1 hour.

7. Let it set for 10 minutes, then serve.

8. If you don't finish the whole thing, don't worry; it's even better as leftovers the next day. Just reheat in the oven at 200°F. It's delicious hot or at room temperature.

AVOCADO TOAST: HOW TO MAKE "WHITE GIRL PIZZA"

Home cooks are never going to pull off pizzeria-quality pizza unless they have a proper oven that gets up to a Satanic 800°F. That's best left to the pros, and you ain't no Paulie Gee. Avocado toast is a perfect alternative. It's natural. It's almost as tasty and melty and decadent as pizza, but you can make it at home without special equipment. Best of all, when it's vegan, it doesn't have to suck.

Three ways to nail it:

1. Smash an avocado and a head of roasted garlic together in a little bowl with salt, pepper, and the juice of 1 lime. Make 2 pieces of toast. Spread the avocado mix on the toast. Cook 2 eggs over medium heat. Top the toast with the eggs. Shake some crushed red pepper flakes on top.

2. Smash an avocado. Hit it with salt and pepper and a pinch of smoked paprika. Spread over 2 pieces of toast. Top with ½ cup peanuts sautéed with Sriracha (or other) chili sauce.

3. Grill some corn (or check out my Elote recipe on page 161). Make your toast, smash your avocado, hit it with some salt, pepper, and chopped fresh cilantro and mix it up. Spread it on your toast, and top with grilled corn and a little hot sauce.

IF YOU DON'T LIKE QUINOA... YOU'RE DOING IT WRONG

Look, I understand your frustration. If I had to eat the quinoa you made, I'd hate it, too. It's not your fault, though. Until this recipe you just didn't know any better. When you throw 1 part quinoa and 2 parts water in a pot and boil that shit for 20 minutes, it tastes like bland nothing. If you overcook it, you end up with a mushy, porridge-like hot mess. Please sir, can I not have some more? It sucks.

Out of everything I learned in culinary school, two things really stuck with me: 1) Everybody looks terrible in a chef's jacket and check pants. Seriously, I went to school with some outrageously attractive people, but didn't realize it until we graduated and I saw them in regular clothes. 2) There is a correct way to make quinoa. And I will share it with you.

---

2 tablespoons butter (Vegans, sub in olive oil or coconut oil.)

1 onion, cut into small dice

½ teaspoon ground cumin (optional, but you should opt in)

1 cup quinoa, rinsed

1¾ cups vegetable broth

Kosher salt and ground black pepper

1. Melt the butter in a small saucepan over medium heat. Throw in the onion with some salt and cumin and stir to coat.

2. Cook that onion until it's brown and caramelized. Resist the temptation to stir it too much—let the heat do the work.

3. Add the quinoa to the pot and stir it in with the browned onions. Give it a minute then add EXACTLY 1¾ cups of broth. It'll get to a boil really quickly. Cover and turn the heat as low as it can go.

4. Cook for EXACTLY 12 minutes. Set a timer.

5. Remove the pot from the heat and let the quinoa sit for 5 minutes.

6. Fluff it with a fork, season with salt and pepper to taste, then hit it with a little oil and stir to combine.

JUST THE TIP: If you have some weird hippie grain and you don't know how to cook it, just boil a pot of water like you were making pasta, throw it in, and check on it every 5 minutes until it tastes ready.

4

TOSS YOUR OWN SALAD

Some jerk once said, "You don't win friends with salad." They obviously don't know me, or what they're talking about. A salad is not an afterthought; it's the main event in a plant-based diet. Salads present infinite possibilities of texture, color, and flavor combinations. Plus, nobody ever got fat from eating too many salads.

When it comes to the definition of a salad, I'm not a stickler. A salad can be the traditional bowl of leafy greens and creamy dressing, crudely chopped vegetables with a squeeze of lemon, mounds of babaganoush and tzatziki with fresh crudités, spiralized raw "noodles"—just about anything comprised mostly of vegetables and fruit. As long as it doesn't involve Iceberg lettuce. Iceberg is a human rights violation as far as I'm concerned, and has no business on your plate.

BIG SALAD WANTS TO KEEP YOU POOR

Do you know how much a chopped salad costs in New York City today? It's $10 for leaves and dressing. If you want actual vegetables mixed in, we're talking $12 to $15. For a salad? That's insane. Think about that—if you order one from the place across the street from your job Monday through Friday for a year, you'll have spent over $3,000 on salad. And that's before buying your artisanal, beard-filtered water to choke it down with.

Stop wasting your money! Why do you need someone to cut vegetables for you? Do it yourself. That's right, I'm telling you to toss your own salad—and spend that three grand on an epic European vacation.

6 OTHER THINGS YOU COULD BUY WITH YOUR SALAD CASH

A bespoke Jack Taylor suit
A Steady Cam HD Video drone (and an extra for after you crash the first one)
A Bottega Veneta leather tote
A refurbished Streetfighter II arcade game
A zero-gravity massage chair
A "date" with your three favorite porn stars

THE RAW VEGAN PAD THAI SALAD CLEANSE

In the Thai language, pad Thai means, "too many greasy noodles for fat Westerners who may or may not be here for sex tourism." So this isn't your typical pad Thai. Instead of a greasy bowl of noodles that will make you want a nap, try a lighter, more refreshing salad made entirely of shredded vegetables. Make it as noodle-like as possible: spiralize, julienne, grate or use a vegetable peeler to create your "noodles." Add a killer tamarind-tahini dressing for the familiar sweet and nutty taste.

1. Combine your shredded vegetables, bean sprouts, and sunflower seeds in a really big bowl and mix them up.

2. Blend in a food processor—or whisk together—the tahini, garlic, tamarind, salt, and pepper to make the dressing.

3. Add the torn cilantro. Dress the salad and toss again.

4. Hit it with some Sriracha.

3 yellow squash, shredded

3 carrots, shredded

1 large cucumber, shredded

3 scallions, shredded

1 cup bean sprouts

½ cup shelled sunflower seeds
(Sub in peanuts for that classic pad Thai crunch, or pistachios if you're rich.)

1 tablespoon tahini

1 teaspoon minced garlic

½ cup tamarind nectar or juice
(You'll find it in Latin and Asian markets.)

Kosher salt and ground black pepper

½ bunch fresh cilantro, leaves torn
(If you're one of those weirdos who tastes soap when you eat cilantro, use basil; Thai basil, if you can get it.)

Sriracha

WATERMELON SALAD

*Vegan

To me, nothing says summer in New York like smelly subway cars, a huge spike in shootings, and watermelon salad made with backyard basil. This version doesn't rely on salty cheese for balance—here, nutritious cashews, kelp noodles, bean sprouts, and a kick-ass spicy Thai dressing allow refreshing watermelon to do its thing.

12 ounces kelp noodles

1 cup cashews

1½ pounds watermelon, cut into large dice

1 cup fresh basil leaves, torn

1 cup crunchy bean sprouts

2 tablespoons sesame oil

2 tablespoons rice vinegar

1 teaspoon Sriracha

1 tablespoon agave nectar (or molasses or whatever sweetener you prefer)

Pinch of adobo seasoning

Pinch of ground ginger

1. Cut the kelp noodles in half and soak in cold water for 10 minutes.

2. In a dry pan over medium heat, toast the cashews until fragrant.

3. Combine the watermelon, basil, toasted cashews, kelp noodles, and sprouts in a large bowl.

4. In a small jar, combine the sesame oil, rice vinegar, Sriracha, agave, adobo, and ginger. Shake until well combined.

5. Pour a little of the dressing over the salad and mix well. (You don't want to overdress it.)

6. Serve. Refrigerate the remaining dressing for dead-easy future salads.

IN PRAISE OF KELP NOODLES

If you're looking to fill up on fewer calories, check out the devil's pasta: kelp noodles. The backstory was outlined in a deleted scene from *The Little Mermaid*—an anthropomorphic young sea kelp waited at underwater crossroads at midnight to make a deal with the devil, exchanging her eternal soul for fame and zero calories. I'm not making this up—kelp noodles bulk up your salad without adding ANY calories. Just don't get hung up on the "noodles" bit. They don't taste like noodles. They don't taste like anything really, just a little salty and crunchy (like the people who enjoy them).

THE WHITEST SALAD YOU'LL EVER EAT: FIDDLEHEADS, KALE, AND PINE NUTS WITH RAMP PESTO

This salad is so white, it probably oppressed your ancestors. This salad is so white, it thinks the cucumber sandwich moving in next door is going to kill property values. If it could wear shoes, they'd be Sperry Top-Siders; if it could dance, it would be embarrassing; if it had Facebook, it would post three times a week about its rescue dog cancer charity 5k. If it went to the beach, it would need SPF 100. If it could complain, it would say, "well why isn't there a white history month?"

To stay true to the theme, I bought all the ingredients at the farmers' market, so we're talking $9 per serving, and the serving size is ridiculously small.

---

1. Start by making the pesto. Chop the ramps and put them all (we're mixing whites and greens) in the bowl of a food processor. Add the olive oil, salt, water, and cheese and pulse until you've made a pesto.

2. Set a large sauté pan over medium-high heat. Throw in the pine nuts until they start to smell toasty, then give them a shake and melt the butter in the pan.

3. Add the fiddleheads and sauté for 3 to 5 minutes until tender but with a bite. (Like how you'd want your asparagus sautéed.)

4. Turn off the heat. Add the baby kale to the pan, and stir in until wilted.

5. Portion the fiddlehead and kale mix out into 4 plates, or 6 plates for super WASPy size. Add a dollop of pesto on top.

1 bunch ramps (wash them well)

¼ cup olive oil

¼ teaspoon kosher salt

¼ cup water

¼ cup Parmigiano-Reggiano cheese

¼ cup pine nuts

2 tablespoons butter

2 cups fiddlehead ferns (Wash them well, too. They can be nasty.)

2 cups baby kale

HELP, MY-VACATION-STARTS-IN-TWO-WEEKS KELP NOODLE SALAD

*Vegan

So, you've got to put on a swimsuit in a couple of weeks but you've been eating like Chris Christie on a bender. Since this salad has such a low-calorie base (hail kelp noodles), I felt free to go nuts adding nuts and seeds. If you have a ripe avocado, throw it in. And for everyone's sake, do some crunches.

1. Soak the kelp noodles in water for 10 minutes. Drain well and use a knife to chop the noodles in thirds.

2. Put the kelp noodles in a mixing owl. Add the carrot, daikon, hemp, sunflower and pumpkin seeds, peanuts, chickpea sprouts, and half of the kale.

3. To make the dressing, combine the remaining kale, shallot, olive oil, water, pine nuts, nutritional yeast, and punch of salt in a food processor. Pulse until you have a pesto. If it's too thick, add more water.

4. Toss the noodle mixture well with ½ to 1 cup of pesto. Save the rest of the pesto in a sealed container for another use.

One 12-ounce package kelp noodles

7 medium carrots, shredded

One 3-inch piece daikon, peeled and shredded

1 tablespoon hemp seeds

1 tablespoon sunflower seeds

1 tablespoon pumpkin seeds

¼ cup peanuts

2 cups chickpea sprouts

4 cups baby kale

1 shallot

¼ cup olive oil

¼ cup water

¼ cup pine nuts

¼ cup nutritional yeast

Punch of kosher salt

MOTEL 6 SALAD

*Vegan

I've never had a Waldorf Salad in my life, though the hotel that invented it is less than twenty blocks away from my apartment. It's one of those watercress-sandwich-without-the-crust foods that never made it across the bridge to Brooklyn. Apparently, it's apples, celery, walnuts, and mayo. Really? A whole Wiki page for that? We can do better.

FOR THE SALAD

½ cup dry wheat berries

1 cup water

½ cup walnuts, toasted in the oven at 350°F for 10 minutes

5 mini cucumbers, sliced

2 cups pitted black olives

2 red bell peppers, seeded and cut into medium dice

2 cups canned white beans, rinsed

2 apples, cored and cut into medium dice

2 cups seedless grapes

FOR THE MOTEL 6 DRESSING

1 cup tahini paste

Juice of 1 lemon

1 garlic clove

1¼ cups water

Kosher salt and ground black pepper

1. Prepare the salad: In a small saucepan combine the wheat berries and 1 cup of water over high heat and bring to a boil. Reduce the heat and simmer for 15 minutes. When done, spread them out on a baking sheet to cool.

2. In a big friggin' bowl, combine the walnuts, cucumbers, olives, bell peppers, beans, apples, grapes, and wheat berries.

3. Make the dressing: In the bowl of a food processor, combine the tahini, lemon, garlic, water, and a pinch of salt and black pepper. Process until it becomes a creamy dressing. If too thick, add more water by the tablespoon.

4. Dress and toss the salad. Refrigerate for 30 minutes before serving.

5. Pour the leftover dressing into a sealed container and use within a week.

GREEN GODDESS SALAD WITH APPLE AND GREEN BEANS

*Vegan

Green Goddess sounds like an environmentally friendly dominatrix or a song about a hot stoner girl, but it's actually a popular salad dressing made with avocado, oil, and mayo that's shockingly unhealthy at 150 calories and 16 grams of fat per 2-tablespoon serving. Sounds innocuous ("green" is good, right?), but it's the Fettuccine Alfredo of dressings. Let's cut the fat and calories and keep the sex appeal.

---

1. Combine all the ingredients for the dressing in a food processor and give it a minute to process. Taste and adjust the seasoning. You're done.

2. Blanch the green beans in salty boiling water for 2 minutes. Run cold water over them until they're cool. Combine with the spinach and apple in a large bowl. Toss with the dressing 1 tablespoon at a time until dressed.

3. Save the extra dressing in a sealed jar and refrigerate.

FOR THE GREEN GODDESS DRESSING

1 cup fresh basil leaves

1 avocado

Juice of 1 lemon

1 shallot

2 tablespoons olive oil

1 tablespoon maple syrup

¼ cup water

Kosher salt and ground black pepper

FOR THE SALAD

1 pound green beans, trimmed

3 ounces spinach

2 apples, cored and sliced

FARRO SALAD WITH PLUMS AND POMEGRANATE SEEDS

*Vegan

I'm obsessed with farro—to the point where I've begun referring to myself as "The Pharaoh of Farro." At least in the kitchen, where I say all sorts of silly things. I think of it as rice, but with Metallica's "Creeping Death" as its soundtrack. A little more substantial and maybe even . . . sinister? It can be used in place of any grain, but I really love it in salad. It works particularly well with citrus and sweet fruits, which you'll find out shortly.

1. In a medium saucepan, sauté the onion with 2 tablespoons of the olive oil over medium-high heat until browned. Add the farro and a pinch of salt and pepper, and stir. Add the water and bring to a boil. Reduce the heat to medium, cover, and cook for 30 minutes. When the farro is done, drain it in a colander and run cold water over it to cool. Set aside in a large bowl.

2. In the same saucepan and working in batches, wilt the spinach over high heat, about 3 minutes. Add the spinach to the bowl of farro.

3. Add the plums, tomatoes, chickpeas, pomegranate seeds, garlic, olives, pistachios, and parsley to the farro and spinach.

4. Toss vigorously with the lemon, the remaining ¼ cup olive oil, and the cumin.

5. Taste for seasoning. Adjust the salt and pepper to your taste.

6. Refrigerate the salad for 30 minutes before serving.

1 onion, cut into medium dice

¼ cup plus 2 tablespoons olive oil

1 cup farro

Kosher salt and ground black pepper

3 cups water

10 ounces spinach

3 plums, roughly chopped

2 vine-ripe tomatoes, sliced

2 cups cooked chickpeas

Seeds of 1 pomegranate (see next page)

½ bulb roasted garlic (sliced in half, wrapped in foil and roasted at 350°F for 1 hour), squeezed

½ cup green olives

½ cup shelled pistachios

1 bunch fresh parsley leaves, chopped

¼ cup fresh lemon juice

1 tablespoon ground cumin

BUILD POMEGRANATE SKILLS

To extract pomegranate seeds like a pro, fill a bowl with water, cut the pomegranate in half, then smack each half on the outside with a wooden spoon over the bowl until the seeds fall into the water. Skim the top of the bowl of gunk; the seeds will fall to the bottom. Drain and eat.

SPICY SYRIAN ROASTED VEGETABLE SALAD

*Vegan

This is my go-to spicy winter starter. The thing that makes it really awesome is the Syrian Seven-Spice blend. It's super spicy, aromatic, and a little sweet. Your kitchen will smell so warm and cozy when you're roasting this that you'll wish you could bottle it and wear it as a scent.

1. Make the spice blend: Mix the spices together and put it in a sealed jar or airtight container.

2. Preheat the oven to 400°F. Line a baking sheet with parchment paper.

3. Prepare the veggies: In a large bowl combine all the vegetables. Sprinkle with a few pinches of the spice blend, give it a glug of olive oil and a punch of salt, then use your gloved (or very clean) hand to toss and combine. The veggies should be coated well and look a little reddish. If not, add more spice, but not too much. It's pretty hot.

4. Place the veggies on the lined baking sheet and roast for 45 minutes.

5. Remove from the oven and set aside until still warm, but not hot, about 10 minutes.

6. Serve over greens.

FOR THE SYRIAN SEVEN-SPICE BLEND
2 teaspoons Aleppo (or cayenne) pepper
1 teaspoon ground black pepper
1 teaspoon ground allspice
1 teaspoon ground cinnamon
1 teaspoon ground nutmeg
1 teaspoon ground coriander
1 teaspoon ground cloves
1 teaspoon ground ginger

FOR THE SALAD
2 zucchinis, chopped
2 sweet potatoes, peeled and chopped
1 pound mini peppers (or chopped bell pepper)
Syrian Seven-Spice blend
Olive oil
Kosher salt
Handful of greens (Whatever's handy. I like arugula.)

ROASTED FINGERLING POTATO AND HERB SALAD

I like a cookout as much as the next guy, but potato salad with mayo is as boring as televised golf. German potato salad is no better. The name sounds like a dodgy sex act, and all you did was put bacon bits and sugar on boiled potatoes. It's time to give potato salad a healthier, tastier upgrade, my friends.

1½ pounds fingerling potatoes, halved lengthwise

5 garlic cloves, pressed or crushed or smashed

Kosher salt

3 tablespoons olive oil

3 scallions, whites and light green parts only, chopped

2 tablespoons champagne vinegar or white wine vinegar

1 teaspoon date syrup (If you don't have date syrup, you can sub in brown sugar or honey, but if you knew what was good you'd have date syrup around.)

½ cup watercress leaves (You can keep a little stem on, but don't make it all stemmy.)

2 tablespoons sliced black olives

1 tablespoon capers, chopped

1 cup fresh basil, roughly chopped

2 tablespoons chopped fresh mint

1 cup fresh chives (about 1 ounce), not so finely chopped

1. Preheat the oven to 425°F. Line a baking sheet with parchment paper or a Silpat mat (a non-stick silicone baking mat).

2. In a medium bowl, toss the sliced potatoes and garlic with a pinch of salt and 1 tablespoon of the olive oil until evenly coated.

3. Place the potatoes and garlic on the lined baking sheet, and turn the potatoes cut side up.

4. Roast until fork-tender and slightly crispy 20 to 30 minutes. I don't know what kind of oven you're working with, so check often after 15 minutes.

5. Combine the scallions, the remaining 2 tablespoons olive oil, the vinegar, and the date syrup in a food processor. Process until it looks and tastes like a vinaigrette.

6. While the potatoes are roasting, combine the watercress, olives, capers, basil, mint, and chives in a large mixing bowl.

7. When the potatoes are done, add to the mixing bowl while still warm.

8. Pour the dressing into the mixing bowl and toss the salad.

9. Taste, and adjust the salt and pepper as needed.

EXTRA CREDIT: If you're not vegan, throw some crumbled feta in there. Any herb you like works here, so use whatever you have at home or get creative. Tarragon, cilantro, and dill all work well.

WASABI-TAHINI BROCCOLI SLAW

Are you a food-waster? Americans throw away about one-third of our available food, and the EPA and U.S. Department of Agriculture are urging citizens to rethink their careless ways. Don't be one of those people who throws out the broccoli stalks and just uses the florets. Those stalks—or what my wife calls "garbage"—are the perfect base for a slaw. One that embarrasses regular-ass cabbage coleslaw by its own basic-ness if you pair it with the right dressing, which we're going to do right now.

1. Using a food processor or a box grater, shred the broccoli stalks and the carrot. Place them in a large bowl along with the shallot and peanuts and toss to combine.

2. In a small bowl, whisk together the tahini, wasabi, water, honey, soy sauce, sesame oil, and vinegar until it forms a smooth dressing.

3. Pour the dressing over the slaw, and mix well.

4. Cover the bowl and refrigerate the salad for a half hour if you have the time. If not, you can serve it immediately.

FOR THE SALAD

2 large broccoli stalks, hard outer layer peeled away

1 carrot, peeled

½ shallot, cut into small dice

½ cup peanuts

FOR THE WASABI-TAHINI DRESSING

1 tablespoon tahini

½ teaspoon wasabi paste

2 tablespoons water

2 teaspoon honey (or agave nectar)

1 teaspoon soy sauce

1 teaspoon sesame oil

1 tablespoon rice vinegar

MOROCCAN EGGPLANT SALAD IN TOMATO SAUCE

This salad is all nightshades, all the time—definitely a no-no on the Tom Brady and Giselle diet plan. Maybe nightshades are inflammatory, and that's why Mediterranean people always seem like they're screaming even when they're happy. It's the tomatoes and eggplant. But, they're so worth it. This salad is what caponata should taste like. Serve it on crostini, heat it up and put it on pasta, use it as a sandwich condiment, or eat it with a spoon.

Canola oil for frying

2 eggplants, peeled and sliced crosswise into ½-inch-thick rounds

1 large onion, diced

4 garlic cloves, sliced

2 teaspoons ground cumin

2 teaspoons smoked paprika

1 teaspoon dried oregano

One 28-ounce can tomatoes with their juice, crushed

¼ cup sliced green olives

1 tablespoon tomato paste

Kosher salt and ground black pepper

1. Heat the canola oil in a large pan over medium-high heat until it shimmers. Add the eggplant slices and fry until soft and browned on each side, about 5 minutes. Transfer the eggplant to a paper towel–lined plate. Repeat until all of the eggplant has been fried

2. Coat the bottom of a saucepan with oil, add the onion, and sauté for 5 minutes. Add the garlic and sauté for 3 minutes. Add the spices, the tomatoes with their juice, and the olives. Simmer and reduce for 15 minutes. Stir in the tomato paste.

3. Increase the heat until the mixture starts to bubble. Add the eggplant rounds and cook for 2 minutes. Remove from the heat, and let cool to room temperature. Using a wooden spoon, break up the eggplant into rustic pieces. Taste and adjust the seasoning if needed

4. Transfer the salad to a container with an airtight lid. Refrigerate overnight.

5. Serve on toasted bread or as a side dish.

RAW, VEGAN, GLUTEN-FREE, LOW-CARB ZUCCHINI "PASTA" SALAD

*Vegan

I know, I know, this recipe sounds about as sexy as going to church. It contains every boring buzzword in the food world. How could it be good? The answer is my vegan pesto. Think of the zucchini as you would spaghetti—minus the carbs and calories you should be saving for beer—merely a carrier for sauce. Buy a Spiralizer so your brain believes you're eating noodles, and you're ready to rock.

1. Make the pesto: Put everything except the zucchini into a food processor and pulse until you achieve a pesto texture. Taste and adjust the seasoning if needed.

2. Prepare the salad: Use a spiralizer to cut the zucchini in a spaghetti shape. (If you don't have a spiralizer, use a vegetable peeler and make thin ribbons or a knife for cutting long matchsticks until it resembles your "pasta" of choice.)

3. Dress the zucchini noodles with ½ cup of the vegan pesto. Save the leftover pesto in an airtight container and use it as a condiment or dressing.

FOR VEGAN PESTO THAT TASTES LIKE PESTO
1 bunch fresh basil (about 2 cups)

1 bunch fresh parsley (about 2 cups)

½ cup walnuts (or use almonds, pistachio, pepitas, anything you like)

3 tablespoons nutritional yeast

2 garlic cloves

1 tablespoon kosher salt

1 teaspoon cayenne pepper (or crushed red pepper flakes)

Finely grated zest and juice of 2 lemons

FOR THE SALAD
2 pounds zucchini, spiralized (about 5 normal-size zucchini)

DOJO-STYLE EAST VILLAGE SALAD

A faithful re-creation of the salad (let's face it, it was the dressing) that brought college students and crusty punks back time and again to Dojo, the cult East Village restaurant. It's also a take on the joint's infamous $3.95 Soy Burger dinner—reborn as a salad—made better and healthier. Plus you won't have to see a rat scamper by while you eat. The clean West Village location is still in business and better than ever.

1. Make the dressing: Combine all the ingredients in a blender or food processor. Add water by the tablespoon if it needs thinning.

2. Prepare the tofu: Preheat the oven to 400°F. Line a baking sheet with parchment paper.

3. In a medium bowl, whisk together all the ingredients for the tofu marinade, except the tofu, until combined. Add the tofu and coat evenly. Spread out on the lined baking sheet and bake for 40 minutes. Remove from oven and let cool.

4. Assemble the salad: Place the greens, cucumbers, pear, baked tofu, and avocado in a large mixing bowl and toss. Add the dressing and toss until evenly coated. Top with sesame seeds.

FOR THE DOJO-STYLE CARROT GINGER DRESSING

1 16-ounce bag baby carrots

2 garlic cloves

Juice of 1 lemon

1 thumb-size piece fresh ginger, peeled and sliced

½ cup canola oil

1 small shallot

1 tablespoon sesame oil

1 tablespoon white miso paste

1 tablespoon mirin (Japanese cooking wine you can find in the supermarket)

1 tablespoon rice vinegar

¼ cup water, plus more if needed

Punch of kosher salt

FOR THE TOFU

1 teaspoon sambal (use Sriracha in a pinch)

2 tablespoons tamari

1 tablespoon sesame oil

1 tablespoon molasses (No molasses? Use honey or date syrup.)

1 tablespoon minced garlic

16 ounces extra-firm tofu, cut into medium dice

FOR THE SALAD

5 ounces greens (whatever you like in your salad)

1 English cucumber, julienned or spiralized

2 Asian pears, cut into medium dice

1 avocado, pitted, flesh scooped out with a spoon

¼ cup Dojo-Style Carrot-Ginger Dressing (above)

1 tablespoon sesame seeds

KIPS BAY REFRIGERATOR KIMCHI

*Vegan

Ever notice that the lines are always longer at the Korean taco trucks than the regular taco trucks? There's one reason for that: The Korean tacos are topped with kimchi, a spicy fermented cabbage condiment that sounds gross but tastes amazing. Just ask a Korean person (or a food-truck foodie).

The traditional way to make it is to bury it underground, but I live in New York so I don't have a yard or the desire to look like a serial killer. This is the fastest, least stinky way to make kimchi—it only needs an overnight in the fridge to magically ferment. I used to sell it out of my kitchen for $15 per quart, but now you can get it for free.

½ **pound daikon radish, peeled and sliced razor thin with a vegetable peeler**

1 **pound napa cabbage, cut crosswise into ½-inch slices**

¼ **cup kosher salt**

1 **thumb-size piece fresh ginger (my thumb is huge, so figure your thumb plus some), minced**

6 **garlic cloves, minced**

1 **bunch scallions, washed well and thinly sliced (use both the white and green parts)**

2 **teaspoons sugar**

½ **cup rice vinegar**

Finely grated zest of 1 lime

2 **tablespoons Sriracha**

1. Fill your biggest pot with water and bring to a boil. Sterilize a quart-size Mason/Bell jar in the water for 15 minutes. Keep the jar in the hot water until you're ready to use it. Do not skip this step.

2. Put the daikon and cabbage in your biggest colander. Add the salt and squeeze it in while mixing well. You want to squeeze the salt in to get the water out of the vegetables. Cover with a towel, then the pot lid, and put a towel or bowl underneath to catch the water. Set aside until wilted, about 2 hours.

3. In a large mixing bowl, whisk together the ginger, garlic, scallions, salt, sugar, vinegar, lime zest, and Sriracha.

4. Fill a bowl with water and dip the wilted cabbage and radish in to remove the salt. Do this 3 times, changing the water each time. Squeeze the excess water out of the cabbage with your (clean) hands.

5. Add the cabbage and daikon to the spicy mixture. Mix well.

6. Fill your jar with the kimchi mixture. Cram it in as tightly as possible so the liquid rises to the top of the kimchi.

7. Clean the lid, and seal the jar—make sure you have it perfectly sealed. (This is really important.) Refrigerate overnight. Now you have kimchi. Remember, it will get spicier and tastier each day that passes.

ELOTE FOR VEGANS

I was lucky enough to have one of life's truly great meals at Elote in Sedona, Arizona. I had almost written off Mexican food entirely until I visited the Southwest. With the zeal of a convert, I ate all the Mexican food in Sedona; it was all awesome, but Elote, a chef-y Mexican-inspired joint with a Dorsia-like wait, was the MVP. Their signature dish is a grilled corn salad, heavy with cheese, chili, and mayo, and I could eat a 55-gallon drum of it, but vegans can't. So I veganized it.

---

1. Get your frying pan hot over high heat. Add the peanut oil. Add the corn and salt and cook for 5 to 7 minutes, stirring constantly, until lightly browned.

2. Remove the corn from the heat and allow to cool.

3. When you're ready to put the salad together (the corn is warm, but not hot), transfer the corn to a medium bowl.

4. Add all the remaining ingredients and stir well to mix.

5. Serve with tortilla chips.

2 tablespoons peanut oil

20 ounces frozen sweet corn kernels, thawed (We're not doing husks-on over a flame, sorry.)

1 teaspoon kosher salt

½ cup Vegenaise (or whatever vegan mayo substitute you like)

¼ cup nutritional yeast

1 teaspoon sugar

¼ teaspoon ground chili pepper

½ teaspoon ground black pepper

Juice of 1 lime

1 teaspoon Cholula hot sauce

Chopped fresh cilantro

MINTED CORN AND AVOCADO SALAD

*Vegan

Sweet corn is everything that's magical about summer, right up there with bikinis, half-day Fridays, and the ice cream truck. This salad tastes like summer in your mouth: a refreshing burst of basil, mint, fresh fava, avocado, and sweet corn. And it's actually good for you. The corn and beans combine to make a complete protein and the avocado provides the good fat. Bring this to a cookout, set it next to the basic corn salad, and watch yours disappear like a Penn and Teller illusion.

---

1. Fill three-quarters of your biggest pot with salty water and bring to a boil. Add the corn and boil for 12 minutes. Remove. Keep the water boiling. Place the corn in a bowl and run cold water over it until cool.

2. Add the fava beans to the boiling water. Cook for 5 minutes.

3. Meanwhile, cut the kernels off the cobs and place in a large salad bowl.

4. Remove the fava beans and run cold water over them until cool. Pop any stubborn beans out of the waxy outer layers if they didn't come off during the boil and add the beans to the salad bowl. Add the cucumber half-moons.

5. In a food processor, combine the avocado, basil, mint, shallot, water, and lemon juice. Process until you achieve a salad dressing texture.

6. Pour the dressing over the salad. Liberally season with salt and pepper—corn, avocado and cukes really love salt, so give it a little extra.

5 ears of corn, husked and silk removed

2 pounds fresh fava beans, shelled

6 mini seedless (or 1 large) cucumbers, sliced into half-moons

1 avocado, pitted and peeled

½ cup fresh basil leaves

½ cup fresh mint leaves

1 shallot

½ cup water

Juice of 1 lemon

Kosher salt and ground black pepper

GREEN BEAN SALAD WITH BLOOD ORANGE JUICE

Don't act like it's not way cooler to make a salad with blood orange juice than regular orange juice from the carton. Anyway, this is a light salad—perfect for lunch or dinner, with a little bit of sweetness, a little bit of spice, and a nice citrus kick.

1. Bring a pot of water to a boil. Add the green beans and cook for 4 minutes. Drain and run cold water over them until they've thoroughly cooled. Set aside.

2. In a large bowl, combine the green beans, salad greens, cucumbers, pear, cannellini beans, a pinch of salt, red pepper flakes, and hemp seeds.

3. Pour the juice and olive oil over the salad. Mix thoroughly. Taste and adjust the salt if needed.

1 pound green beans

2 cups salad greens

6 mini seedless cucumbers, or 1 large seedless, sliced into half-moons

1 pear, cut into medium dice

2 cups cannellini beans

¼ teaspoon crushed red pepper flakes

¼ cup hemp seeds (any seed or nut will do)

Juice of 2 blood oranges

Glug of olive oil

Kosher salt

"KOHL(RABI)SLAW" WITH APPLE, CUCUMBER, AND MISO-DILL DRESSING

`*Vegan`

So, it turns out you like it raw. When I asked you guys on Facebook what kind of recipe you wanted to see in the book, one universal answer was "a low-carb, vegan, raw summer salad." Enjoy!

FOR THE SALAD

4 heads kohlrabi, peeled

2 apples (Like Danny Zuko in *Grease*, I prefer Pink Ladies.)

2 large cucumbers

Juice of 1 lemon

½ cup shelled sunflower seeds

¼ cup hemp seeds

¼ cup flaxseeds

1 tablespoon sesame seeds

Kosher salt and ground black pepper

FOR THE MISO-DILL DRESSING

1 bunch fresh dill, washed, bottom half of stems removed

2 tablespoons white miso paste

2 tablespoons olive oil

1 garlic clove

1 piece of peeled fresh ginger (about the same size as the garlic clove)

½ cup water

1. Prepare the salad ingredients: Shred the kohlrabi, apples, and cucumbers using the shredding attachment of a food processor or an old-fashioned box grater. Place the grated fruit and veggies in a large bowl. Drizzle with the lemon juice (so that the apple doesn't get all brown and gross) and mix to combine.

2. Make the dressing: Combine the dill, miso, oil, garlic, ginger, and water in the bowl of a food processor. Pulse until it becomes a delicious dill dressing and sticks to your finger or tasting spoon, about 1 minute.

3. Dress the slaw with the miso-dill dressing. Mix in the seeds. Taste and adjust the seasoning.

MANGO TANGO TIKI SALAD

Was it Jesus or MLK who said, "the only certainties in life are death and taxes"? I'd like to add one more: Your meal at a tiki bar and restaurants will certainly always suck. Those menus are based on some rum-soaked World War II vet's notion of what Polynesian food should taste like. Over sixty years have gone by, but the food hasn't improved. So I booked a ticket to Tiki Oasis, the biggest annual Tiki festival in the U.S., and made it my mission to fix "Tiki" food. Light your torches, throw on a Hawaiian shirt, invite your friends over for strong-ass drinks, and serve this. Everyone will be happy. Except for "cultural appropriation"-obsessed SJWs. They're never happy unless they have something to be outraged about.

1. In a large bowl, combine the sambal, maple syrup, and liquid smoke and mix well. Add the tofu pieces and toss to coat. Set aside.

2. Combine all the shredded fruit and veggies in a bowl.

3. Preheat a grill pan and grill that tofu. Pour about half of the marinade over the tofu. Grill it until the outside is crispy on all sides. Set aside.

4. Combine the olive oil, the remaining marinade, and fruit nectar to make your dressing. If you're feeling adventurous, deglaze the grill pan with a little juice and add all that spicy, smoky awesomeness to the dressing. Mix well and dress the salad. Serve the salad with tofu and black sesame seeds on top.

5. This makes a lot. If you want to save some, drain it in a fine-mesh sieve, cover, and stick it in the fridge. (It makes a killer sandwich filling.)

3 tablespoons sambal (You can sub in any chili sauce or paste here.)

1 tablespoon maple syrup

2 teaspoons liquid smoke

1 package extra-firm tofu, cut into strips (Make the effort to press the water out first.)

1 small red cabbage, shredded

1 pound carrots, peeled and shredded

1 shallot, shredded

1 mango, peeled, pitted, and shredded

1 cucumber, shredded

¼ cup olive oil

¼ cup passion fruit nectar (or use any tropical fruit you have handy)

Black sesame seeds

"SESAME-SILANTRO" SOBA SPRING SALAD

Shockingly substantial, this sweet supper salad showcases spinach, soba, and sliced strawberries. Say that five times fast, dickus.

1. Bring a pot of salty water to a boil. Add the fava beans and cook until all the beans float to the top, about 5 minutes. Using a strainer, remove the cooked beans and run cold water over them until cooled. Keep the water in the pot boiling.

2. Combine the spinach, tomato, strawberry, apple, and beans in a large salad bowl.

3. Add the soba noodles to the boiling water and cook for 5 minutes. Drain in a colander. Run cold water over the noodles to cool and rinse them. (See the tip below.)

4. Combine the cilantro, garlic, vinegar, and oil a food processor and process until it becomes a dressing. Pour it into one of those hipster Mason jars.

5. Add the soba to the salad. Pour half of the dressing into the bowl and mix well. Garnish with sesame and pomegranate seeds. Keep the extra dressing for a future salad.

2 cups fresh or frozen fava beans (Edamame are a good substitute.)
3 cups fresh spinach
2 cups cherry tomato, halved
1 pint strawberries, sliced
2 apples, cored and sliced
4 ounces fresh soba noodles
1 bunch fresh cilantro
1 garlic clove
⅓ cup rice vinegar
½ cup sesame oil
½ teaspoon black sesame seeds
Pomegranate seeds (optional)

JUST THE TIP: SECOND-TO-NONE SOBA SECRET: The key to good soba is the cold water wash. The shock of cold stops the noodles from continuing to cook (and getting flaccid). Move the noodles around with the water running as if you're washing them in an old-timey miner's village.

GREEN SALAD WITH WARM SPICY LENTILS

*Vegan

This salad hits every one of your taste buds—sweet, sour, savory, spicy, and smoked—and it works as a balanced, protein-packed dinner. If nutritionists actually cared about the taste of food, this is what they'd recommend.

FOR THE SALAD

2 cups dried green, brown, or
  French Puy lentils

1 tablespoon hot paprika

1 tablespoon smoked paprika

3 hearts romaine, chopped

2 cups chopped spinach leaves

8 ounces hearts of palm, chopped

¼ cup olives (the good ones, not
  the crappy little green ones with
  pimientos)

¼ cup flaxseeds

¼ cup pickled green peppercorns
  (I can see you rolling your eyes
  from here. You can also sub in
  capers.)

2 apples, sliced

FOR THE DRESSING

½ cup olive oil

Juice of 2 lemons

1 tablespoon Dijon mustard

1 teaspoon maple syrup

Kosher salt and ground black
  pepper

1. Fill a large saucepan with 4 cups of water, the lentils, and both paprikas. Bring to a boil, cover, and simmer for 35 minutes. Drain to remove any excess liquid. Set aside.

2. Combine the veggies, fruit, and seeds in a large bowl. Top with the warm paprika-spiced lentils.

3. Whisk the oil, lemon juice, mustard, and maple syrup together in a bowl. Add salt and pepper to taste. Pour some over the salad to dress, then save the rest in a jar. Toss the salad and serve.

TOASTED PITA AND SESAME SEED SALAD WITH DRIED FRUIT

*Vegan

I'm a huge fan of dried fruit, and you should be, too. I sometimes fantasize about going to the Dried Fruit Association's yearly convention like a cosplayer. I'd dress up like a California Raisin and get my picture taken with the titans of the dried fruit industry. The rest of the world may still call them prunes, but I was really into that "Plum Amazin" rebranding. I might have been the only one.

---

1. Combine all the ingredients in a large bowl and toss.
2. Taste and adjust the seasoning if needed.

1 pita, toasted until crispy as a chip and broken into pieces

2 hearts of romaine, chopped

1 large cucumber, sliced

4 radishes, sliced

½ cup pitted green olives

2 scallions, thinly sliced

½ cup sunflower seeds, toasted in the oven at 350°F for 10 minutes

¼ cup golden raisins

4 dried figs, diced

Juice of 1 lemon

Splash of good olive oil

Kosher salt and ground black pepper

FRUITY REMEMBER-WHEN-IT-WAS-SPRING SALAD

In a post–climate change world, spring is nothing more than a fantastical notion from the past. (Like Atlantis, reliable American-made cars, and cigarettes that are good for you.) Let's make spring a state of mind and enjoy this refreshing, hydrating salad in the sweltering heat or frigid cold, or from an underwater abyss caused by a full-on polar ice cap meltdown.

2 tablespoons olive oil

1 tablespoon white wine vinegar

1 teaspoon agave nectar (Honey or maple syrup work fine, too.)

3 ounces spring mix salad greens

3 Persian cucumbers, chopped

2 cups strawberries, hulled and sliced

2 pears, cored and cut into medium dice

2 cooked veggie burger patties, crumbled

1 bunch fresh mint leaves, chopped

12 ounces grape tomatoes, halved

Kosher salt and ground black pepper

1. Whisk together the oil, vinegar, and agave until it forms a dressing. Set aside.

2. Combine the remaining ingredients in a large salad bowl. Dress and toss. Taste and adjust the salt and pepper if needed.

PINCHE GRINGO ENSENADA con CILANTRO VINAIGRETTE

I've said it before, but it bears repeating: It is impossible to get good Mexican food in NYC. I've been as disappointed as a virgin on her wedding night at every supposedly "authentic" Mexican spot. I've eaten at the Red Hook soccer tacos, the place in Staten Island where they serve goat eyes, the place inside the auto body shop, the place under the tortilla factory, the *Top Chef* version of Mexican cuisine, every joint in Jackson Heights, Corona, and Sunset Park . . . and they're all garbage compared to the worst taco stand in San Diego. If you want it done right (on Eastern Standard Time), you're going to have to do it yourself.

---

1. Put all the ingredients for the dressing in a food processor. Process until you have a dressing.

2. Place all the ingredients for the salad in a large bowl. Dress with half of the cilantro vinaigrette and toss. Save the remaining half in a covered container for another use.

FOR THE CILANTRO VINAIGRETTE

1 bunch fresh cilantro, leaves
  picked

¼ cup fresh lime juice

⅓ cup canola oil

1 teaspoon ground cumin

1 teaspoon molasses

2 tablespoons hot sauce (I like
  Cholula Chipotle)

FOR THE SALAD

4 ounces baby spinach

2 cups black beans, drained and
  rinsed

2 cups canned corn kernels or
  hominy

1 red bell pepper, seeded and
  diced

1 avocado, pitted, peeled, and diced

UNSPECIFIED-NATION-OF-ORIGIN MIDDLE EASTERN SALAD

*Vegan

I've always known this as an Israeli salad, but apparently, Persians, Turks, and the Lebanese also claim it as their own. So, if your country is full of dudes with a massive amount of chest hair who only button their shirts halfway, you're probably familiar with this salad. It's super easy, super low calorie, and can be eaten with breakfast, lunch, dinner, or as a snack.

1 seedless cucumber, peeled, cut into small dice

3 vine-ripe tomatoes, cut into small dice

½ medium red onion, cut into small dice (Like, smaller than small. Imagine you're a person who hates chewing and wishes everything had the texture of hummus.)

1 bell pepper (red, orange or yellow is best—green gets a little bitter), seeded and cut into small dice

A glug of extra-virgin olive oil

Finely grated zest of 1 lime

Juice of 2 limes

10 green olives, chopped

½ cup chopped fresh parsley

Generous amount of salt and ground black pepper

1. Prep all the vegetables and add to a large bowl.

2. Dress with the olive oil, lime zest, and juice.

3. Add the olives and parsley and mix thoroughly. Season with salt and pepper.

4. Cover the bowl and refrigerate the salad for 30 minutes.

5. Serve and eat while chain-smoking and yelling into your cell phone.

ARUGULA SALAD WITH GRAPES, GORGONZOLA, AND TOASTED PECANS

This is my go-to basic salad. The sweetness of the grapes balances out the strong flavor of the gorgonzola and shallots. Toasted pecans make everything awesome. My mom and my sister-in-law, Shira, love it, and I love them—but I always forget to give them the recipe. Here it is.

FOR THE SALAD

4 ounces baby arugula

½ cup pecans, toasted in the oven at 350°F for 10 minutes, or in a dry pan until they smell delicious

1 pint cherry tomatoes, halved lengthwise

Handful of seedless red grapes, halved

1 small shallot, minced

1 bell pepper (red, orange, or yellow), seeded and cut into medium dice

2 ounces crumbled gorgonzola cheese

FOR THE BALSAMIC DRESSING

⅓ cup red wine vinegar

½ cup good-quality olive oil

1 teaspoon Dijon mustard

1 teaspoon honey or maple syrup

Pinch of kosher salt and ground black pepper

1. Mix all the ingredients for the salad in a large bowl.

2. Make the dressing: Combine all the ingredients in a jar with a cover. Whisk together with a fork. Shake the jar to recombine when ready to use.

3. Dress the salad with less than half of the dressing and toss to combine.

4. Cover the dressing jar and save for another time.

KICK IT UP: Like I said, this is my basic, go-to recipe. When it feels tired, I add any or all of these for a little change of pace: more cheese, pear slices, chopped celery, Granny Smith apple, or cucumber slices.

5

LAZY ONE-POT MEALS FOR WHEN YOU JUST CAN'T

L

ook, everyone knows that the worst part of cooking is washing the dishes afterwards. I hate doing dishes so much that I eat off of paper plates when nobody is coming over. (Sorry, Al Gore.) It's enough that I made dinner! Why do I have to get prune hands at the sink, too? Here are a few of my favorite dishes with maximum taste and minimal cleanup.

SUSHI RICE MOROS

*Vegan

This was a happy accident. I was craving rice and beans, but the only rice I had in my cupboard was sushi rice. So I said, Fuck it, I'll make Cuban moros using polished Japanese rice because nothing is sacred. My version is as authentic to Latin-Caribbean cuisine as Taco Bell is to Mexican food, but it's delicious. You can feed an army with it or have leftovers for days.

---

1. Heat 2 tablespoons of the olive oil in a large saucepan over medium-high heat.

2. Add the onion, pepper, garlic, thyme, oregano, and adobo. Add the tomato paste and stir to combine. Let it sauté for 2 minutes until fragrant.

3. Throw in the olives and beans and stir to combine. Cook for 1 minute.

4. Add the broth and bring to a boil. Add the rice and the remaining 2 tablespoons olive oil and let cook, uncovered, for 5 minutes.

5. Cover the pan and allow to simmer on the lowest heat setting for 15 minutes. Turn the heat off, keep covered, and let it sit for 5 minutes.

6. Uncover and stir in the cilantro. Taste and check for seasoning. Add salt if needed.

¼ cup olive oil

1 onion, cut into small dice

1 green bell pepper, seeded and chopped (You can use red or orange or yellow peppers, too.)

2 garlic cloves, minced

½ teaspoon dried thyme

½ teaspoon dried oregano

1 tablespoon adobo seasoning

¼ cup tomato paste

1 cup green olives, whole and pitted

2 cups black beans (that's one fifteen-ounce can of beans, drained and rinsed)

2½ cups vegetable broth

2 cups sushi rice (Regular white rice works, too.)

½ bunch fresh cilantro, leaves chopped

Kosher salt

POLAR VORTEX POTATO CASSEROLE

When it's 25 degrees below and there's a foot of snow outside, you're not motivated to go food shopping. This is my take on what a homemaker who lived in a flyover state and didn't feel like digging out her car made for dinner during long winters in the '60s and '70s. It's comforting, creamy, starchy, filling, and delicious. The perfect meal to energize you for a key party.

1 teaspoon olive oil

1 onion, thinly sliced

1 tablespoon butter

1 cup whole milk

1 can cream of mushroom soup

3 potatoes, peeled and thinly sliced (⅛ inch) on a Mandoline or the side of a box grater (Slices should look like really skinny American footballs.)

1 cup veggie crumbles (or grate/ crumble some veggie burgers or tempeh)

½ cup Parmigiano-Reggiano cheese

Kosher salt and ground black pepper

Truffle salt/truffle oil/truffle butter . . . just, truffle something

1. Preheat the oven to 425°F.

2. Heat the olive oil in a small saucepan on medium heat. Add the onion along with a pinch of salt and sauté for 5 minutes. Remove from the heat.

3. Combine the butter and milk in a small saucepan. Heat until the butter has melted, then whisk in the cream of mushroom soup until combined.

4. Place half of the sautéed onions in the bottom of a 9-inch baking dish. Cover the onions with a layer of sliced potatoes. Cover the potatoes with the veggie crumbles and ¼ cup of the cheese. Pour half the cream of mushroom mixture over.

5. Top the mushroom mixture with a layer of potatoes, and then repeat the same layering process again. Cover the whole thing with the rest of the cream of mushroom mixture.

6. Bake for 35 to 40 minutes until the top has browned.

7. Serve with a pinch of truffle salt, a splash of truffle oil, or a thin pat of truffle butter.

TRY THE TIP: Make it vegan by using 1¼ cups mushroom soup instead of anything with cream or butter, and sub Daiya for cheese.

CAN-CAN CHEAP-ASS CHILI

Not every vegan is interested in paying a month's rent for a week's worth of groceries at the greenmarket. Supermarkets often have sales on canned goods, and that's the best time to stock up. (Who doesn't get a little excited every year the first time they hear the ShopRite "Can Can Sale" jingle?) Regardless of what the Internet says, everything from a can isn't toxic poison. Sure, canned goods often use preservatives and can be a little salty. By all means, rinse them first. But do not be can-shamed. Say it loud: "I don't always want to soak my beans overnight then boil them for 2 hours—sometimes I just want to open a goddamn can and heat up my dinner like they did during World War II."

1. Say a small prayer to the BPA gods as you open all your evil cans and packages. Dump the contents in a large pot and stir it up.

2. Add ½ cup of water and bring to a boil. Reduce the heat and simmer for 45 minutes.

3. Scoop out the avocado flesh by the tablespoon and stir in.

4. Add a handful of shredded Daiya (if using) and melt it into the chili.

5. Serve the chili over rice and stretch your dollar even further. It should make 10 to 12 meals for less than $20.

One 8-ounce can tomato paste

1 tablespoon adobo seasoning

One 7-ounce can chipotle peppers in adobo sauce (Rinse first if you're not a hot-food hero.)

One 20-ounce can kidney beans, drained and rinsed

One 10-ounce package frozen spinach

One 12-ounce package veggie ground beef substitute (I like Morningstar Farms Grillers Crumbles.)

One 16-ounce can hominy (or regular corn kernels)

1 ripe avocado

Daiya nondairy cheese, Pepper Jack type (optional)

CURRIED SEITAN AND OKRA STEW

*Vegan

I picked up this recipe from a Rastafarian dude who threw whole Scotch Bonnet peppers, one of the world's hottest varieties, into his okra stew. I'm not going to do that because I don't want to kill you people, I just want to feed you. Ya know, Rastas are about more than just smoking ganja and hating on white devils. They follow strict dietary guidelines that promotes natural, organic, and mostly plant-based foods—oddly, there's a clause about being able to eat fish under six inches long. It's called Ital food, which isn't short for Italian. It's short for Vital, though not that much shorter. Now you know.

---

2 tablespoons coconut oil

2 leeks, washed thoroughly and thinly sliced

One 1-inch piece fresh ginger, peeled and minced

1 pound small red potatoes, halved

1 pound okra, chopped

8 ounces seitan, cubed

1 tablespoon curry powder

1 teaspoon ground turmeric

3 shakes hot sauce

2 cups tomato puree

4 cups water

1 tablespoon cornstarch

Kosher salt and ground black pepper

1. In a large soup pot, melt the coconut oil over medium heat.

2. Add the leeks, ginger, and a pinch of salt and stir to combine. Sauté for 3 to 5 minutes.

3. Add the potatoes, okra, seitan, curry, turmeric, hot sauce, tomato, and water, with a punch (not a pinch) of salt and bring to a boil. Reduce to a simmer and cook, covered, for about 30 minutes. After 30 minutes.

4. Add the cornstarch. Reduce the heat to the lowest setting. Cover and cook for another 30 minutes. Taste for seasoning and adjust as needed.

BULGUR WHEAT AND GREEN PEAS

You can't eat rice and beans every day, though lord knows many of us have tried. (We were young and broke.) It's time to mix things up. Here are a few cool facts about bulgur wheat: it has fewer calories, less fat, and loads more fiber than even brown rice. It's also endlessly entertaining to hear some people pronounce it "burgle" (burghul) because it makes me think of the Hamburglar burgling someone's pantry.

1. Melt the coconut oil in a large saucepan over medium heat.

2. Add the leek and a pinch of salt. Stir and sauté for 3 minutes.

3. Add all other ingredients except for the water and stir to combine. Cook for 3 minutes.

4. Add the water and bring to a boil. Lower the heat to the lowest setting, cover, and simmer for 20 minutes.

5. The water should be totally absorbed by the bulgur. Taste and adjust the seasoning as needed.

2 tablespoons coconut oil

1 leek, cleaned and sliced thinly into half-moons

2 teaspoons kosher salt

1 tablespoon ground turmeric

Juice of 1 lemon

1 tablespoon sumac

1 tablespoon fenugreek

1 cup dry bulgur

2 cups frozen peas

¼ cup tomato paste

2 cups water

RED HOT KIMCHI UDON NOODLE SOUP

If the way into a man or woman's pants is through their stomach, this soup ought to spice things up right quick. Think of it as the Agent Provocateur of Japanese noodle soups. And it's almost as easy as your mom. (Kidding! Your mom is a very nice lady who is not at all promiscuous. What I mean is, it's almost as easy as making Instant Ramen.)

---

1 onion, diced

2 cups kimchi (see Kips Bay Kimchi, page 160)

6 cups vegetable broth

9 ounces vegan "chicken" (I like Beyond Meat or tofu.)

1 tablespoon white miso paste

1 pound udon noodles

1. Sauté the onion and kimchi in a large pot until they start to get . . . uh, fragrant. If you have a roommate, they'll probably peek their head out to find out what that fermented cabbage smell is.

2. Add the broth, fake meat, and miso. Stir to combine.

3. Cover and let simmer for 20 minutes.

4. Bring a pot of water to a boil. Throw in the udon noodles and cook for 3 minutes. Drain.

5. Divide the noodles among four bowls and ladle the soup on top.

MO ROCKIN' BEAN SOUP

I always make a big batch of this soup in the winter because it tastes even better the next day. It's a warming and filling dish that covers all of your nutritional bases and makes you feel cozy.

1. Cover the bottom of a big soup pot with olive oil and place over medium heat. Add the onion and garlic and cook until the onion is soft and the garlic becomes fragrant.

2. Add everything else and bring to a boil. Reduce to a low simmer. Cover and cook for 45 minutes.

3. Taste and adjust the seasoning if needed.

> **JUST THE TIP:** Don't kill yourself trying to find the right ingredients. Soup and stew-making is all about working with what's handy. No crushed tomato? Use fresh ones, tomato sauce, whatever you have. Swap kidney beans for basically any legume, Israeli couscous for any grain, kale for spinach, mustard or collared greens. It all works in soup.

Olive oil

1 large onion, small dice

8 garlic cloves, minced

One 28-ounce can crushed tomatoes

Three 15-ounce cans kidney beans

½ cup Israeli couscous

2 sweet potatoes chopped

One 10-ounce package frozen kale

32 ounces vegetable broth

1 tablespoon ground cumin

1 teaspoon ground cinnamon

1 teaspoon sweet paprika

½ teaspoon crushed red pepper flakes (if you like it spicy, add more)

Kosher salt and ground black pepper

BANGIN' BAINGAIN CURRY

`*Vegan`

My neighborhood borders an area called Curry Hill—the Indian section of Murray Hill. It's an embarrassment of amazing vegetarian restaurants (even Jain ones), specialty stores, and spice markets. One Friday night, I was about to order Baingain Bartha from our go-to delivery spot Dhaba, when I had a sudden attack of frugality. Instead of spending $35 on delivery for two, I realized I could order FIVE movies on demand—the ones that are still in theaters, something I consider the ultimate luxury—and be entertained all weekend. There was also the added bonus of choosing my own spice level.

3 small eggplants, cut into medium dice

2 pounds tomatoes

1 big-ass onion

6 garlic cloves

One 1-inch piece fresh ginger, peeled

2 teaspoons garam masala

1 teaspoon ground cumin

1 teaspoon ground turmeric

1 teaspoon smoked paprika

1 teaspoon curry powder

1 teaspoon ground fenugreek

1 pound okra, sliced into 1-inch rounds

½ cup almonds

2 cups sweet peas

2 cups chickpeas

½ cup water

1 bunch fresh cilantro, chopped

Kosher salt

1. Preheat the oven to 400°F. Roast the eggplants whole for 15 minutes. Set aside and, when cool enough to touch, chop into bite-size pieces.

2. Combine the tomatoes, onion, and garlic in the bowl of a food processer. Process until you have a smooth-ish cooking base (no big chunks).

3. Pour the cooking base into a large saucepan and place over medium heat. Add the ginger and spices to the pot and stir it up.

4. Add the chopped eggplant, okra, almonds, sweet peas, chickpeas, and water and stir to combine. Simmer for 30 minutes.

5. Taste and adjust the seasoning. (You'll probably need salt here.)

6. Garnish each bowl with the chopped cilantro.

7. This makes 10 to 12 servings. It's awesome hot over rice or quinoa or cold on a piece of bread like an "Indian-ish" bruschetta.

THE BEST LENTIL SOUP

My grandmother made the best chunky Italian lentil soup in the world, so I always felt like a traitor when I'd order my second-favorite lentil soup—the spiced, pureed version from Turkish spots like Bereket on NYC's Lower East Side (RIP) and Sahara on Coney Island Avenue in Brooklyn. When left to my own devices, I like to combine the ingredients of both (yup, basil *and* coriander) and give it a half-assed puree to reach a texture somewhere in the middle. This recipe serves, like, 20 plus. If you're trying to save some loot, portion it out and freeze it. Now you have 20 super-cheap, ready-to-go meals.

1. Coat the bottom of the biggest stockpot you have with olive oil and place over medium heat. Throw in the onion, carrot, basil, celery, and garlic and stir to coat with the oil. Hit it with a handful of kosher salt. (I'm serious about the handful as a measurement.) Sauté, stirring, for 10 minutes.

2. Add the lentils, sausage, tomatoes, and spices. Sauté, stirring, for 3 minutes.

3. Add the broth and bring to a boil, then add the spinach. Keep it at a boil for 3 minutes. Reduce to a simmer. Cover and simmer for 1 hour.

4. Give it a taste. If a flavor needs bumping up, add some more; if it needs to be thinned out, add some water. If it's good, leave it alone.

5. Using a hand blender, puree the soup. (Do a little or a lot, or not at all. What do I care?)

6. Let it sit for 15 to 20 minutes. Ladle into bowls and top each with a couple shakes of nutritional yeast.

Olive oil
2 gigantic onions, cut into small dice
1 pound carrots, peeled and cut into small dice
1 bunch fresh basil, pulsed in food processor or chopped
1 bunch celery hearts, chopped
10 garlic cloves, minced
Kosher salt
12 ounces dried lentils (brown or green)
1 12-ounce package Lightlife or Field Roast Italian-style grain "sausage," chopped
16 ounces diced tomatoes
1 tablespoon ground cumin
Kosher salt and pepper
½ teaspoon crushed red pepper flakes
1 teaspoon ground coriander
1 teaspoon smoked paprika
8 cups vegetable broth
One 10-ounce package frozen spinach
Nutritional yeast

EASY PEASY GREEN SOUP

This pureed pea soup is one of those dishes that tastes like it took a long time to make, but in reality you need less than 20 minutes. Basil and garlic do most of the heavy lifting flavorwise, while green peas provide vibrant color. It's bright and nutritious, and goes really well with grilled cheese sandwiches.

2 tablespoons coconut oil

1 large red onion, diced

3 garlic cloves, sliced

1 piece fresh ginger about the size of your pinkie, peeled and sliced

3 celery stalks with their greens, sliced

Kosher salt and ground black pepper

3 cups frozen green peas

4 cups vegetable broth

1 bunch fresh basil leaves

Sliced almonds

1. Melt the coconut oil in a large pot over medium heat. Swish it around to cover the bottom.

2. Add the onion, garlic, ginger, celery, salt, and pepper. Cook for 5 minutes, or until soft and fragrant.

3. Add the frozen peas and cook for another 5 minutes.

4. Add the broth and basil. Let simmer for 5 minutes more.

5. Carefully ladle the soup into a blender and puree. (Do this in batches so the blender doesn't shoot hot soup all over your kitchen.)

6. Taste and adjust the seasoning if needed.

7. Garnish with basil leaves and almond slices.

WINO STEW

*Vegan

Don't get this confused with hobo stew—that's a totally different thing you cook over a campfire while someone plays a rusty harmonica and watches for coyotes. This stew is just as simple to make, but red wine and aromatics give it a pseudo-French sophistication.

Olive oil

2 onions, sliced

5 garlic cloves, minced

Punch of kosher salt

1 pound carrots, chopped

1 large eggplant or 2 small eggplants, chopped into bite-size pieces

1 cup pearled barley

8 ounces mushrooms (baby bella or button), sliced

8 ounces seitan, chopped

2 tablespoons dried thyme

1 tablespoon dried basil

2 teaspoons ground black pepper

2 cups red wine

2 cups vegetable broth

2 tablespoons tomato paste

2 zucchini, sliced into half-moons

One 14-ounce can butter beans, drained and rinsed

½ cup water

1. Coat the bottom of your biggest pot with olive oil and place over medium heat. Add the onions, garlic, and salt and stir to coat. Cook for 5 minutes.

2. Add the carrots, eggplant, barley, mushrooms, seitan, thyme, basil, and pepper. Stir and cook for 5 minutes more.

3. Pour the wine and broth in, increase the heat, and bring to a boil. Reduce to a simmer, and stir in the tomato paste. Cover the pot and cook for 45 minutes.

4. Add the zucchini, butter beans, and ½ cup of water (but only if the liquid has mostly evaporated). Stir, and cook for an additional 15 minutes.

5. Turn off the heat and let it sit for 10 to15 minutes before serving.

YELLOW SPLIT PEA SOUP

*Vegan

Usually the split peas you see in soup are green. I chose yellow ones here because the Goya aisle was sold out of the green ones. It makes no difference—they taste identical and I always side with the underdog. You usually get some smoky ham flavor in a traditional split-pea soup, and I didn't want to lose that. That's where the smoked tempeh comes in. Close your eyes and it tastes just like traditional green split pea soup made with ham hock, but it's not.

1. Coat the bottom of a large soup pot with olive oil and place over medium-high heat.

2. Add the onion and a punch of salt and pepper. Stir to coat with the oil. Sauté for 5 minutes. Add the garlic and sauté until fragrant.

3. Add the tempeh, carrots, celery, adobo, turmeric, cinnamon, and paprika and stir to combine. Sauté for 5 minutes, or until the vegetables are tender and there's a strong bacon-like smell.

4. Add the split peas and stir to combine.

5. Add the vegetable broth and bring to a boil. Reduce to a simmer, cover, and cook for 1 hour.

6. Turn off the heat. Using an immersion blender (or a regular blender, working in batches), puree the soup.

7. Taste and adjust the seasoning if needed.

Olive oil

1 large onion, cut into medium dice

Kosher salt and ground black pepper

10 garlic cloves, sliced

6 ounces Lightlife Organic Fakin' Bacon Tempeh Strips (or any fakin' bacon)

½ pound carrots, peeled and chopped

6 celery stalks, chopped

1 tablespoon adobo seasoning

1 tablespoon ground turmeric

½ teaspoon ground cinnamon

2 teaspoons hot paprika

1 pound yellow split peas

12 cups vegetable broth

AVOCADO MASHED POTATOES

And, since you asked, no, I don't get tired of eating vegetables.

---

1 head garlic, roasted in the oven for 1 hour at 350°F

3 potatoes, peeled and quartered

1 ripe avocado

Kosher salt and ground black pepper

2 tablespoons unsweetened almond milk

1. Boil the potatoes in a large pot until fork-tender, about 15 minutes. Drain in a colander, and return the potatoes to the pot.

2. Squeeze the roasted garlic and avocado flesh into the pot. Season with a bunch of salt and pepper.

3. Mash that all together and add the almond milk to help the consistency and make this the best vegan mash you've ever had. Who needs cream and butter when you have avocado and roasted garlic?

> **JUST THE TIP:** If you don't have enough time (or interest) to roast garlic—shame on you—you can still make this dish by with a shake of adobo in place of the garlic.

(LOW CARB) RAMEN WITHOUT THE RAMEN

*Vegan

There are plenty of vegetables in the sea, and they're full of nutrients, not simple carbohydrates. I'm going to show you how to use them to make one of our favorite comfort foods into something healthful. This version of ramen is for people who want to enjoy a "noodle-y" soup without all the starchy noodles.

1. Soak the kelp noodles in a bowl of warm water for at least 10 minutes.

2. Brush the seitan with the mustard, and lightly coat with the panko.

3. Place a sauté pan over medium-high heat, coat the bottom with oil, and pan-fry the seitan until crispy, 5 to 7 minutes. Transfer to a plate lined with a paper towel to absorb excess oil. Set aside.

4. Add the broth, water, scallions, kombu, sesame oil, soy sauce, mirin, rice vinegar, and kelp noodles to a really big soup pot and stir it up. Simmer over medium heat for 20 minutes.

5. Throw in the bean sprouts and carrot. Fill your bowls and slurp.

6 ounces kelp noodles

8 ounces seitan, cubed

2 tablespoons Dijon mustard

½ cup panko bread crumbs

Canola or vegetable oil

4 cups vegetable broth

4 cups water

1 bunch scallions, sliced

1 cup kombu (that's the seaweed restaurants use for seaweed salads) cut into strips that kinda-sorta look like noodles

2 tablespoons sesame oil

2 tablespoons soy sauce

2 tablespoons mirin

1 tablespoon rice vinegar

½ pound bean sprouts

1 carrot, spiralized

GRILLED BROCCOLI RABE

At an NYC Italian-American street fair, sausage and pepper heroes are for suckers and tourists. One of my favorite things in the world is the broccoli rabe sandwich they also serve at the sausage and pepper stands. You can either make this as a standalone side dish or grill up some Italian bread, spread some roasted garlic on it and do it right.

1. Get a pot of water boiling, add the broccoli rabe, and blanch for 1 minute.

2. Meanwhile, get a large grill pan hot over medium heat.

3. Remove the broccoli rabe from the boiling water with tongs (don't shake it dry) and place it in a bowl with the olive oil, adobo, and red pepper flakes. Mix everything together.

4. Drop the broccoli rabe onto the hot grill pan, making sure every inch is touching the hot surface. Cook for 4 to 5 minutes until charred, then drizzle with a little balsamic vinegar to prevent burning.

5. Using tongs, flip it to the other side. Place the cheese over the broccoli rabe so it melts evenly, covering it. Cook for another 4 to 5 minutes until it's charred on the opposite side and the cheese has melted.

1 bunch broccoli rabe, the tough lower parts of the stems removed

2 teaspoons olive oil

1 teaspoon adobo seasoning

½ teaspoon crushed red pepper flakes

1 to 2 teaspoons balsamic vinegar

2 ounces fresh mozzarella cheese, diced (you can use the grated stuff, too)

GARAM MASALA SWEET POTATOES

These spiced sweet potatoes are packed with beta-carotene, vitamin C, B-vitamins, and fiber. If your pants feel tight lately, know that this dish is low-fat and pre-portioned by Mother Earth. Squint real hard and they look like restaurant potato skins. The tops are crisped like a potato chip, and the bottoms are soft and spicy. "It tastes like Thanksgiving in India." –my wife.

Cooking spray

3 medium sweet potatoes (the orange ones), peeled and sliced very thinly. (If you have a mandoline or a box grater with the side part for scalloped potatoes, use it.)

3 tablespoons melted coconut oil

2 tablespoons garam masala

1½ teaspoons kosher salt

1. Preheat the oven to 400°F. Spray a 12-cup muffin pan with the cooking spray.

2. In a large bowl, combine the sweet potato slices, coconut oil, garam masala, and salt. Using your clean hands, toss everything together, making sure the potatoes are evenly coated.

3. Fill each of the cups in the muffin pan with slices of sweet potato until they're just overflowing.

4. Roast for about 45 minutes. Taste one. The top should be slightly charred and the bottom should be fully cooked.

SAUTÉED SPINACH WITH BREAD CRUMBS

Here's another classic side dish from the Brooklyn region of Italian cooking. A bag of frozen spinach costs $2.50 in the supermarket and yields six portions; if you tried to do the same thing with the fresh spinach they sell as salad greens, it would cost ten times as much. The bread crumbs not only add flavor, they soak up any extra moisture from the frozen spinach.

Olive oil

6 garlic cloves, sliced Goodfellas-thin

Punch of kosher salt

One 20-ounce bag frozen spinach, defrosted

½ teaspoon lemon juice

½ teaspoon crushed red pepper flakes (Use less if you're a hot food wuss.)

½ teaspoon raisins

1 cup bread crumbs (any kind you like, seasoned or plain, panko or homemade)

1. Cover the bottom of a large pan with olive oil and place over medium heat. Add the garlic slices and the salt. Stir and sauté for 2 minutes, or until fragrant.

2. Add the spinach, lemon juice, red pepper flakes, and raisins; keep stirring and cooking for 5 minutes more.

3. Stir in the bread crumbs and cook for 2 minutes more.

4. Taste and adjust the seasoning if needed.

6

THE SWEET SPOT: DESSERTS THAT AREN'T ENTENMANN'S

wasn't always a dessert guy. In fact, I blame one man for my current sweet tooth: Osama Bin Laden. One night early in 2002, when I was still a cop, I was smoking a cigarette near the flaming hole in the ground where the World Trade Center once stood. I was shooting the shit with a fireman when a backhoe kicked a cloud of dust into the air. He suggested we put our respirator masks back on, so I put out my cigarette and we did. The machine, stuck behind some heavy debris, tugged on a piece of rebar. Suddenly, it pulled the reinforcing rod free—it swung loose and smashed me right in the face. I had a concussion and a broken nose.

Thanks to that fireman, I kept my teeth. Thanks to the rebar, I got a month off work.

Long story short, while I was recovering from reconstructive surgery, nose packed with yards of gauze, I wasn't able to taste a goddamn thing. My entire face was swollen, and everything tasted like blood or nothing at all. My wife started bringing me pints of ice cream because the only thing I could taste in that pitiful condition was sweetness. Now, I love dessert as much as anyone else; probably even more. Here are some of my favorites—some are guilt-free, some are decadent, and all are worth the broken nose.

RAW-VEGAN "NOT-ELLA"

*Vegan

Nutella is everything that's wrong with today's NomNom culture. Slather it on toast, a crepe, a pizza, a shoe, or eat it with your filthy finger out of the jar—then take a picture, tag it #nomnomnom and watch the likes roll in. The only problem? That shit ain't food. It's an expertly-branded tub of gross chemicals, MSG, palm oil, and artificial flavors designed to trick you into believing you're eating chocolate-hazelnut spread on toast. If you want something done right, you gotta do it yourself. That's just what I did here, with all-natural raw, vegan* ingredients.

1. Place all the ingredients in a high-powered blender or food processor and blend until you have a smooth, spreadable consistency. This might take a few minutes; be patient.

2. Spread it on some good bread.

3. Instagram it and make sure the lighting is good, douchebag. Lighting is key.

4. Eat, and watch the likes roll in.

1 cup hazelnuts, soaked overnight

10 ounces pitted dates, soaked for 30 minutes to rehydrate

¼ cup date syrup (you can use maple syrup, but it might taste a little "pancake-y")

½ cup coconut milk, plus more if needed

¼ cup raw cacao powder

2 teaspoons vanilla bean paste (or pure vanilla extract)

*Store-bought Nutella contains (non-vegan) whey and skim milk. Also, Santa Claus isn't real.

GRADY'S COLD BREW CHOCOLATE AND PECAN BREAD PUDDING

In this role-playing scenario, I'll be your dessert-slinging Paula Deen, but without N-word and secret diabetes. This pudding was inspired by one of her recipes, but my version mixes Greenpoint, Brooklyn, with Savannah, Georgia. Southern pecans and melty chocolate chips give this bread pudding a brownie vibe, and Grady's chicory-infused coffee concentrate adds another dimension of taste. (Imagine me saying that in a Rod Serling voice while wearing a blonde wig. Because now I'm Paula Deen doing Rod Serling.)

1½ cups heavy cream

1 cup whole milk

½ cup Grady's Cold Brew coffee concentrate*

2 cups granulated sugar

¼ cup unsweetened cocoa powder

1 tablespoon pure vanilla extract

1 teaspoon ground cinnamon

4 large eggs, beaten

½ cup chopped pecans

8 ounces of your favorite chocolate, chopped

1 pound day-old Italian or country white bread, cut into 1-inch cubes (Leave out on the countertop overnight.)

1. Preheat the oven to 350°F. Grease a 9 x 13-inch baking dish.

2. In a large bowl, stir together the cream, milk, and Grady's Cold Brew concentrate.

3. Add the sugar, cocoa, vanilla, and cinnamon to the mix and stir until incorporated.

4. Stir in the eggs, pecans, and chocolate.

5. Add the bread to the prepared baking dish. Cover with the liquid mixture. Let the bread absorb the liquid for 30 minutes.

6. Bake for 1 hour. By then, the bread pudding should be set and moistened by melted chocolate.

7. Serve hot, cold, or at room temperature.

*Theoretically, you could replace Grady's Cold Brew concentrate with another sub-par brand made by someone who isn't nearly as cool as Grady (full disclosure: he's a friend of mine). You can also use instant cappuccino dissolved in water, but you won't get that unique kick of chicory.

COCO-MANGO FLAN "CHEESECAKE"

Vegan cheesecakes have let me down more often than the New York Mets (and I've lived through three decades of their incompetence). I always hope for the best, but I know it's going to suck. Since I can't become the general manager of the Mets, I'll do my part by making a decent vegan cheesecake. Instead of trying to replicate a slice of Junior's, I let the ingredients be their best selves. This crustless cheesecake is kind of like a firmer version of flan, and it tastes like coconut and mango. You'll love it and your friends will think they're eating something made with cream and eggs. You don't even need to tell them it's vegan. It can be made in advance in only 10 minutes.

---

1 mango, peeled and sliced

One 14-ounce can unsweetened coconut milk

2 teaspoons pure vanilla extract

½ cup sugar

½ cup cornstarch

Coconut oil (optional)

Ground cinnamon

1. Place the mango, coconut milk, vanilla, sugar, and cornstarch in a blender or food processor and puree the hell out of it until it's well combined.

2. Pour it into a saucepan and place over medium heat. Cook, stirring frequently with a wooden spoon, until it thickens and coats the spoon.

3. Grease a 9-inch round baking dish with a little bit of coconut oil and pour in the custard. (You could also fancy it up by dividing the mixture among six individual ramekins or small bowls.)

4. Refrigerate for at least 4 hours, or until it sets.

5. Slice and serve.

MATZO HALVAH TRUFFLES

My mother-in-law makes a similar dessert for Passover, but hers is an artfully arranged layer cake. I'm not trying to win any beauty contests, so I turned her concept into the popcorn shrimp of Judaism—I want to pop as many of these things in my mouth as possible, year-long. Seriously, these little balls of halvah, matzo, and chocolate are so good that if they were served at Middle East peace talks, something might actually get done.

1. Melt the chocolate in a double boiler.

2. Put the halvah in a medium saucepan over medium heat. Melt it a little, and then add the cocoa, sugar, and water, stirring frequently. Cook until melted and fully incorporated.

3. Add the butter and Grand Marnier to the halvah fudge and stir to combine.

4. Pour the melted chocolate in and stir until fully incorporated.

5. In a large bowl, thoroughly coat the matzo with the chocolate-halvah sauce. Cover and refrigerate for 30 minutes.

6. Scoop out a heaping tablespoon at a time and roll into a rustic ball. Place each ball in a mini cupcake liner and refrigerate until you're ready to serve.

10 ounces chocolate (a mix of dark and milk works best)

8 ounces halvah, crumbled

3 tablespoons unsweetened cocoa powder

3 tablespoons sugar

¼ cup water

½ pound (16 tablespoons/2 sticks) butter or vegan butter substitute

2 teaspoons Grand Marnier

10 pieces matzo, broken into small pieces

MAPLE-CINNAMON CHIA PUDDING

As a superfood, chia seeds are the best thing since hummus and krill oil, according to that cardiac surgeon/snake-oil-selling clown, Dr. Oz. Unlike most things that come out of his mouth, this one is actually true: the little guys are packed with fiber, omega-3s, protein, and tryptophan, and they make you feel really full, really fast—which is pretty great for those of us who need to lose a chin or two. (Plus, they make a way better dessert than hummus and krill oil.)

½ cup chia seeds

2 cups almond or coconut milk

3 tablespoons maple syrup

1 teaspoon ground cinnamon (use the real stuff)

1 teaspoon pure vanilla extract (use the real stuff)

½ cup strawberry puree (just puree ½ cup of strawberries)

1. Get a quart-size jar—or one of those Chinese take-out soup containers—and put everything in except the strawberry puree.

2. Stir it up. Cover it, shake it really hard, then refrigerate for at least 6 hours. (Overnight is better.)

3. To serve, portion it out in a bowl, and top with a spoonful of strawberry purée.

GRILLED PINEAPPLE

You don't have to know the first thing about cooking to master grilled pineapple. A pineapple is delicious on its own. Add cinnamon and coconut oil, then allow the natural sugars to caramelize over a fire, and you've got something really special.

---

1. Using a sharp knife, cut the pineapple into quarters, making sure to cut around that hard core and throw the core out.

2. Cut the skin away and slice each quarter in half lengthwise for 8 peeled pineapple wedges.

3. Get a grill pan really hot.

4. Shake some cinnamon over the pineapple wedges. Rub it into the wedges until they are coated.

5. Melt your coconut oil in the hot grill pan. Drop the pineapple on the hot grill pan and grill for 4 minutes per side.

1 whole pineapple*
½ teaspoon ground cinnamon
2 tablespoons coconut oil

*Did you know that in New York City's Eataly market, Mario Batali's Italian-themed grocery food court, there is a person whose job title is Vegetable Butcher? You can either read my two-sentence instruction on how to cut your pineapple, or you can go there and defer to a professional and feel like a schmuck-on-wheels (alternately, a "job creator").

IRISH BISCUIT CAKE

When you're visiting Ireland, forget about Guinness. The only dark stuff you should be shoving down your throat is chocolate biscuit cake. It's easily my favorite dessert in the entire world, and I have no idea why Americans haven't caught on. It's the easiest thing in the world to make and you can customize it and make a different version every time. I've been to Ireland a bunch of times, but it wasn't until two punk rock chicks were selling slices of this at a farmers' market that I jumped into the biscuit cake game.

---

1. Combine the chocolates and coconut oil in a medium pan over medium heat. Stir until melted. Remove from the heat.

2. Stir in the condensed milk to thicken the mixture.

3. Add the biscuits, nuts, and fruit and stir until they're evenly covered in chocolate.

4. Line a loaf pan with parchment paper. You might want to give the parchment a spritz of cooking spray.

5. Pour the mixture into the loaf pan. Using a spoon, press the top down so it's level.

6. Refrigerate until it's fudgy and set, about 4 hours.

7. Slice and serve.

3 ounces dark chocolate, broken up

8 ounces milk chocolate, broken up (spend a little extra for the good stuff)

½ cup coconut oil

One 14-ounce can sweetened condensed milk

8 ounces butter cookies, broken up (They're called biscuits in Ireland and the UK. I like Leibniz or Lu brands, or you can go traditional with McVitie's or go wild and use Ritz crackers.)

¼ cup sliced almonds (Use any nut you want here.)

¼ cup raisins (or any other dried fruit, or no dried fruit at all)

STRAWBERRY ICE CREAM YOU CAN MAKE IN YOUR FRIDGE

Here are the ingredients in a pint of premium "natural" strawberry ice cream: Milk, Skim Milk, Cream, Sugar, Strawberries, Strawberry Revel (Sugar, Strawberries, Water, Natural Strawberry Flavor, Pectin, Blue 1 and Red 40, Phosphoric Acid, Citric Acid, Malic Acid), Corn Syrup, Mono & Diglycerides, Carob Bean Gum, Guar Gum, Natural Strawberry Flavor, Carrageenan, Cellulose Gel, Cellulose Gum.

If that's what you want to eat, don't let me stop you. Enjoy your corn syrup, gums, and gels. Or you could try my ice cream with normal people ingredients. All you need is a strong blender and a working freezer.

---

4 cups strawberries

1 cup whole milk

1/3 cup sugar

¼ teaspoon ground cardamom

½ teaspoon pure vanilla extract

Shredded coconut for garnish

1. Wash the strawberries. Cut the green parts off, put into a covered container or resealable freezer bag and freeze. (Stick them in the freezer before work in the morning and they'll be ready in time for dessert.)

2. In a powerful blender—I use a Vitamix—combine the frozen strawberries, milk, sugar, cardamom, and vanilla. Blend on low until the mixture begins to incorporate.

3. Increase speed slowly until you reach the high setting and blend until you've got ice cream in there. It should take around 30 seconds—you want ice cream, not a milk shake. (See below.)

4. Scoop it out and garnish with coconut.

5. Crazy, right?

TRY THE TIP: If your blender's being a dick, or seems like it's stuck and the ingredients aren't blending, turn it off and use a wooden spoon to clear the area around the blades. Then, push the unblended top part to the bottom and try again. You might have to do this a few times. And buy a better blender.

FROZEN MANGO LASSI

The best dessert in an Indian restaurant is something they think is a drink—the sweet mango lassi. They make a salty one, too, but that sucks. The sweet one is like a classic milk shake that's heavy on the mango flavor (and heavy on your stomach, since they give you about a pint-glass's worth at a time). When my server brings it over, I always wish it was in ice cream form. Or frozen yogurt. Maybe in a cone? So I made my own version. You decide how you feel about the cone; it's not my business.

---

1. Place all the ingredients in the bowl of a food processor. Process until completely combined. Scrape down the sides and process for 1 minute more.

2. Pour the mixture into a freezer-safe container, cover it, and place in the freezer for 1 hour.

3. Remove the frozen yogurt from the freezer and stir it. Break up any large frozen chunks, making sure the texture is smooth. Cover and return it to the freezer for 2 to 3 hours until a soft-serve texture is achieved.

4. Serve the frozen yogurt in bowls, dividing it equally, and grate some fresh apple on each for garnish. (You can also freeze it overnight, remove from the refrigerator and thaw for 20 to 30 minutes before serving.)

2 ripe mangoes, peeled and cubed

4 cups plain, full-fat yogurt

1 cup sugar

2 teaspoons pure vanilla extract

¼ teaspoon kosher salt

1 apple (I like Granny Smith.)

> **JUST THE TIP:** This recipe makes a lot of frozen yogurt. Luckily, it refreezes well. Eat within 5 days, though, or freezer-burn will strike.

BROWN SUGAR SLUSHY

In Italy, they call this a granita, which sounds pretty upscale. (The Italian word for milk is *latte*, so they're known for this type of thing.) It's got the semifrozen texture that put 7-11 on the map. In my version, the flavor is a mix of sweet and tart. I came up with this for a client who had a sophisticated palate and really enjoyed a slushy now and then, but wouldn't be caught dead in a strip mall.

1 cup brown sugar

2 cups water

2 pears, cored and chopped

Juice of 2 lemons

1. In a small saucepan over medium heat, dissolve the brown sugar in the water. Simmer for 4 minutes, whisking throughout. Remove the pan from the heat and let cool to room temperature.

2. Combine the sugar water, pears, and lemon juice in a blender. Blend until completely pureed.

3. Place a fine-mesh strainer over a square, freezer-safe container. Strain the blend until the liquid is in the container and the pulp is in the strainer.

4. Save the pulp. That's homemade pear sauce! (Think applesauce, but with pears.)

5. Place the container in the freezer for 1 hour. Ice should form around the edges. Using a spoon, scrape the sides and pull the frozen bits towards the center.

6. Repeat every hour until it reaches a slushy-like consistency. (It should take about 5 hours total. Don't make plans.)

7. Serve in chilled glasses.

YELLOW SNOW (AKA FROZEN LEMONADE)

As far as I can recall, the most worthwhile piece of advice anyone has ever given me was, "don't eat the yellow snow." But that just made the idea of yellow snow a forbidden fruit (or frozen dessert in this case), so I turned it into a zesty, honey-infused frozen lemonade that's sweet enough for dessert, and strong enough to fight onion or garlic breath.

---

1. Whisk together all the ingredients in a large bowl.

2. Fill 2 ice cube trays with the liquid and put in the freezer until frozen.

3. Remove the ice cubes when frozen (less than 5 hours) and place in a blender. Blend until you achieve a frozen snow consistency.

4. Scoop and serve.

Finely grated zest of 2 lemons

1 cup fresh lemon juice (about 8 lemons, juiced)

2 cups water

2 tablespoons honey

PEANUT BUTTER–ACAI BOWL

This is basically a sundae that's so good for you, you can eat it for breakfast or dessert. It's an antioxidant powerhouse, combining strawberry, blueberry, and acai to destroy free radicals, and peanut butter and coconut shavings for some good fat to sustain you.

Two 3.5-ounce packages frozen acai

1 ripe banana (overripe is even better)

1 cup blueberries

1 cup strawberries

1 cup seedless red grapes

½ cup unsweetened coconut flakes

1 cup coconut water

1 cup muesli (that's granola for Europeans)

4 tablespoons smooth peanut butter

Sliced strawberries

Blueberries

1. Blend the acai, banana, berries, grapes, and coconut flakes with coconut water until smooth.

2. Fill four bowls with the acai mixture.

3. Top with muesli, peanut butter, and berries.

CITRUS OLIVE OIL CAKE

This is the perfect dessert for people who aren't into overly sweet treats. It's great after dinner with an espresso, or in the morning with a cappuccino. Maybe it sounds a little weird to you, but by this point in the book you should trust me.

1. Preheat the oven to 350°F. Grease an 8-inch cake pan with olive oil.

2. Combine the eggs, vanilla, orange zest, sugar, and olive oil in a mixing bowl and whisk together until combined. (A hand mixer would be nice here.)

3. In a separate bowl, mix the dry ingredients together and add them to the wet ingredients. Whisk the hell out of it until you have a smooth batter.

4. Pour the batter into the prepared pan, and bake the cake for 35 minutes or so.

5. Check it with a toothpick in the center. If it comes out clean, you're done. If not, give it 5 minutes more.

6. Remove from the oven and let it cool. Serve warm or at room temperature.

5 large eggs

½ teaspoon pure vanilla extract

Finely grated zest of 2 (normal size) oranges

1½ cups sugar

2 cups really good olive oil

1½ cups all-purpose flour

2 tablespoons cornstarch

Pinch of kosher salt

1 teaspoon baking powder

BALSAMIC STRAWBERRIES

Darryl Strawberry was my favorite baseball player when I was a kid. From time to time, I still get the old jingle for the cheesy girl store at the mall stuck in my head. ("Have you shopped Strawberry today?") Anyway, this is the easiest old Italian lady dessert you'll ever make. The pepper might seem totally out of place here but it makes sense once you taste it, so don't start thinking about leaving it out.

1. Place all the ingredients except for the yogurt in a large bowl. Stir and mix well.

2. Cover and refrigerate for at least 2 hours, or until the balsamic vinegar and sugar form a syrup.

3. Serve with a dollop of Greek yogurt. (Vegans, this is great with almond-based yogurt.)

8 cups strawberries, sliced
½ cup balsamic vinegar
½ cup sugar
¼ teaspoon ground black pepper
1 cup Greek yogurt

TRY THE TIP: Save your leftovers and use as a topping for oatmeal, pound cake, or angel food cake.

MORE THAN THE TIP: If a guest is coming over, serve it with Cannoli Cream (page 222) instead of yogurt and watch them freak out.

CANNOLI CREAM

Fruit salads are cool and all, but when you start spooning cannoli cream on top, you go from the person who was trying to pass off fruit as dessert to a kitchen rock star. Best of all, it couldn't be easier to make.

½ cup full-fat ricotta cheese

½ cup heavy cream

⅓ cup powdered sugar

¼ teaspoon ground allspice

½ teaspoon ground cinnamon

1 teaspoon chocolate chips, chopped

1 teaspoon finely grated orange zest

1. Using an electric mixer, or a whisk if you have strong arms, beat the ricotta until smooth.

2. In a separate bowl, combine the cream, sugar, allspice, and cinnamon. Whisk until you have firm peaks. (You'll want that electric mixer for this unless you're The Mountain from *Game of Thrones*.)

3. Fold in the ricotta mixture. Stir in the chocolate chips and orange zest.

4. Throw it in the refrigerator for at least an hour.

5. Put in on anything and it'll make it better: fruit, cake, between two cookies, on a cupcake, in a cupcake, on toast to make the toast taste like cake.

CHOCOLATE-COCONUT-BANANA PUDDING

If you want to trick your kids (or an uncooperative adult) into eating more nutritious foods, I've found it helps to hide them in chocolate. This mousse is rich and chocolaty, and totally vegan. Moms dig it, and you know how I feel about moms. (See chapter one)

1. In a blender or food processor, puree the avocado, banana, cocoa, vanilla, coconut milk, and Splenda until it looks like chocolate mousse.

2. Refrigerate for at least 1 hour.

3. Garnish with coconut flakes and a chocolate square, and serve.

1 very ripe avocado (Choose one that's soft to the squeeze with dark green skin, not one that feels like a rock.)

1 ripe banana (with leopard spots)

¼ cup cocoa powder (Use the good stuff: unsweetened Dutch cocoa has tons of antioxidants, maaaaan.)

1 tablespoon pure vanilla extract

⅓ cup unsweetened coconut milk (Any nut milk works here; I just like coconut best.)

3 packets Splenda (I'm chubby and trying to change that. If you're not into artificial sweeteners, use 3 packets of Stevia, 2 tablespoons sugar, date syrup, agave nectar, or whatever you usually use.)

Toasted coconut flakes

1 square raw chocolate

THE BEST RICE PUDDING EVER

This is a very inappropriate story for me to tell in a cookbook. (Sorry.) If you're squeamish, I suggest just skipping down to the recipe.

While testing this super-tasty, super-rich recipe, I ended up with a huge amount of this stuff. I gave some to my neighbors, my doorman, a homeless dude in the street, and I still had enough left over to fill a pint-size container, which I gave to a friend we'll call Dave. Dave is a very physically fit guy who is always training for some kind of charity Iron Man nonsense. He was feeling a little peckish on his long bike ride to meet the Tinder date of his dreams, so he pulled over to have a taste—and wolfed down the whole pint. He met his date and they got to chatting, but that didn't last long. He literally ran away from her . . . and into the Union Square public bathroom, where he experienced a humbling bout of gastric distress.

"I know I shouldn't have eaten it all, but it was so gooooood," he moaned to me on the phone later that night. "I can never talk to her again. But it was worth it." The moral here is portion control. Serve it a half-cup at a time.

8 cups whole milk

One 6-ounce can sweetened condensed milk

1½ teaspoons pure vanilla extract

1 cup Arborio rice

4 tablespoons (½ stick) unsalted butter

½ cup sugar

Pinch of kosher salt

4 large eggs, beaten

2 ounces dark chocolate, grated

1. Combine the milk, sweetened condensed milk, vanilla, rice, butter, sugar, and salt in a medium saucepan. Bring the mixture to a boil over medium-high heat. Reduce the heat to low and simmer for about 40 minutes, uncovered, stirring every few minutes. If the rice isn't fully cooked, give it more time until it is.

2. Whisk in the beaten eggs and cook for 1 minute. The pudding should coat the back of your spoon.

3. Remove the pan from the heat and let the pudding cool to room temperature.

4. Refrigerate and serve cold. Sprinkle grated chocolate on top.

REGULAR CHEESECAKE FOR REGULAR PEOPLE

Sometimes you don't want to make things too complicated with cardamom pods or matcha tea dust. This is the perfect crowd-pleasing, middle-of-the-mall dessert you can bring to a dinner party with people you don't know very well and still come off like a hero.

1. Make the crust: Preheat the oven to 350°F. Grease a 9½-inch springform pan.

2. Mix together the graham cracker crumbs and melted butter until the crumbs are moist. Press the crumbs into a layer that covers the bottom of the prepared pan.

3. Bake the crust for 10 minutes. Set aside to cool.

4. Make the cheesecake: Add the sugar and vanilla to the cream cheese and mix until smooth.

5. Add the eggs and crème fraîche and mix until smooth.

6. Pour the batter over the cooled graham cracker crust.

7. Bake the cheesecake for 1 hour. It should move like a good burlesque dancer—a little jiggly.

8. Let cool to room temperature. Then refrigerate for at least 5 hours before serving.

FOR THE CRUST
1 cup graham cracker crumbs (6 to 7 graham crackers)
2 tablespoons unsalted butter, melted

FOR THE CHEESECAKE
1 cup sugar
1 tablespoon pure vanilla extract
3 cups cream cheese, softened
3 large eggs
1 cup crème fraîche

NOT QUITE DESSERTS

Sometimes you want something sweet, and an apple won't cut it. If you're trying to eat clean, you're not left with very many options. That's when you'll be happy to have a batch of these "muffins" on hand. They work as a breakfast, a snack, or a dessert that's not really a dessert. All of them are vegan, under 100 calories, and sweet enough to satisfy a craving. Plus, they're made of oats so they're substantial enough to stave off a binge.

100-CALORIE BAKED OATMEAL "MUFFINS"

*Vegan *Low-cal

Warning: These may look like muffins, but don't let appearances trick you into thinking these are some kind of indulgent dessert. They're portable, single-serve oatmeal thingies that are shaped like muffins: Easy, beyond healthy, and only around 100 calories each.

I make one or two batches per week, and my wife and I eat them for breakfast or for a post-gym or afternoon snack with a cup of coffee. I've made 36 different versions of this recipe—past versions have included yogurt, eggs, quinoa, pumpkin, quick-cooking oats, steel-cut oats, Dutch cocoa, coconut flakes, hemp milk, soy milk, Amish milk, blueberries, Craisins, blackberries, nutmeg, and cardamom (but not all together). Anyway, this one is the best, aka "The Classic."

---

2 medium ripe bananas (spotty, not those pale yellow ones that taste like a potato)

½ cup unsweetened applesauce

3 packets Stevia (use honey, maple syrup, sugar or nothing)

2½ cups quick-cooking rolled oats (the old-fashioned 5-minute kind)

2 teaspoons ground cinnamon

1 teaspoon pure vanilla extract

6 Medjool dates, pitted and chopped

½ cup raisins

1 teaspoon coconut oil, plus extra for greasing the pan

2 cups unsweetened almond milk (Get Blue Diamond brand if you can.)

12 hazelnuts (Walnuts, cashews, or pecans work, too.)

1. Preheat the oven to 400°F. Grease a 12-cup muffin pan with coconut oil.

2. In a large mixing bowl combine the bananas, applesauce, and sweetener. Using a potato masher or a fork, mash until smooth.

3. Add the oats, cinnamon, vanilla, dates, raisins, coconut oil, and almond milk. Mix until fully combined, but a little soupy.

4. Using a spoon, fill each of the cups with the mixture. Top each with a hazelnut.

5. Place in the oven and bake for 30 minutes (or longer if your oven sucks).

MIX IT UP: Replace the dates and nuts for new flavor combinations, such as blueberries and walnuts, date and coconut flakes, shredded apples and walnuts, Craisins or dried cherries and pecans, cocoa powder, cinnamon, and walnuts ("The Rugelach"), or just say fuck it and add chocolate chips like you really want to.

PUMPKIN-SPICE OAT MUFFINS

*Vegan   *Low-cal

Look, every fucking thing doesn't have to taste like pumpkin spice come autumn. That chemically altered-to-taste-like-pumpkin-spice latte ruined the whole damn season with its popularity. Now everybody has to get in on the act. At this point, I'm certain that Babeland (or your local sex toy store) will roll out edible panties and dental dams once the leaves start changing. I blame omnipresent pumpkin spice for the rise of Donald Trump (look at that pumpkin orange face). Thanks for nothing.

That said: these are 77-calorie pumpkin-spice muffins with natural ingredients.

1. Preheat the oven to 400°F. Spray a 12-cup muffin pan with cooking spray.

2. Combine all the ingredients in a blender. Blend until it becomes a batter.

3. Fill the holes of the prepared pan with the batter.

4. Place a pecan half on top of each. (They look adorable.)

5. Bake for about 20 minutes, or until a toothpick comes out clean.

Calories:

Pumpkin: 80

Applesauce: 100

Banana: 105

Oats: 380

Molasses: 210

Almond milk: 60

Divide that by 12 and you have 77.

Cooking spray

1 cup organic pure pumpkin puree (not pumpkin pie filling)

1 cup unsweetened applesauce

1 cup quick-cooking rolled oats (the old-fashioned 5-minute kind)

⅓ cup molasses

2 teaspoons ground cinnamon

½ teaspoon ground cloves

½ teaspoon ground nutmeg

1 tablespoon vanilla bean paste (or pure vanilla extract)

½ teaspoon baking soda

1 cup unsweetened almond milk

12 pecan halves

PEANUT BUTTER–BERRY OATMEAL MUFFINS

`*Vegan`   `*Low-cal`

A delicious, portable protein-powered breakfast or snack for around 100 calories without all the preservatives of a protein bar. Yeah, it's pretty awesome.

1. Preheat the oven to 400°F. Grease a muffin pan.

2. In a large mixing bowl, combine the applesauce, sweetener, vanilla, peanut butter powder, water, flaxseeds, oats, and berries. Stir well and let sit for 5 minutes.

3. Using a spoon, fill each of the cups with the mixture.

4. Place in the oven and bake for 30 minutes.

TRY THE TIP: Dust your berries with a little bit of flour before adding, so they don't just sink to the bottom of the muffin like they're wearing cement shoes.

Cooking spray

1 cup unsweetened applesauce

4 packets Stevia (or your favorite sweetener)

1 teaspoon pure vanilla extract

2 tablespoons PB2 (this brand of peanut butter powder is great for using in smoothies, sauces, and oat muffins)

2 cups water

2 tablespoons flaxseeds

2½ cups quick-cooking rolled oats (the old-fashioned 5-minute kind)

2 cups raspberries (or any kind of berry)

COCOA-COCONUT-OATMEAL MUFFINS

I get more e-mails about Baked Oatmeal "Muffins" (page 228) than any other recipe. Apparently, people are really into the idea of natural 100-calorie breakfast muffins. I get it, but what about something a little sweeter? What about a guilt-free dessert for when you know you have no business eating dessert? Let's make it happen with two things everyone loves: coconut and chocolate.

Cooking spray

1 banana, mashed

2 cups quick-cooking rolled oats (the old-fashioned 5-minute kind)

1 cup sweetened shredded coconut, plus extra for topping

2 cups coconut almond milk (Any nut milk works here.)

½ cup cocoa powder (It's not really dessert if it's not chocolaty.)

⅓ cup agave nectar

1 tablespoon coconut oil

1½ teaspoons pure vanilla extract

1. Preheat the oven to 400°F. Spray a 12-cup muffin pan with cooking spray.

2. Mix everything together in a large bowl. Stir it like you mean it.

3. Fill the cups with the batter. Top with shredded coconut.

4. Bake for 30 minutes, or until they can pass the toothpick test.

STONER PANINI

Once, I was testing recipes from a famous Italian chef whose recipes were always perfect. I invited three friends over for what was sure to be an incredible meal, and it was. Her recipes were creative, delicious, and not overly complicated. The meanest-spirited Yelp reviewer couldn't find fault with anything served. The last dish to come out was a kid-friendly panini that looked kind of insane: It mixed melted cheese with raspberries, rosemary, and brown sugar.

My guests went crazy for it. It turns out that they were all high, and "kid friendly" was also code for "stoner friendly." I don't even smoke weed, but I loved it, too. The rest of the night turned into an unexpected ingredient grilled cheese party. The following recipes are the keepers. (Each makes 4 sandwiches.)

FRIED HALLOUMI WITH APPLE AND HONEY

Why do paninis have to even have bread, maaaaan? (Well, *pane* = bread in Italian, but whose counting?) Halloumi is a Greek cheese that's meant to be grilled. Genius.

One 8-ounce block halloumi cheese

2 apples, thinly sliced (Use a mandoline if you have one, or a box grater or peeler if you don't.)

Honey

Freshly ground black pepper

1. Slice the block of cheese lengthwise into 8 thick slices.

2. Preheat a grill pan over medium heat.

3. Top 4 pieces of cheese with apple slices, a drizzle of honey, and a crack of black pepper. Cover those with the remaining 4 slices of cheese so it looks like a small sandwich.

4. Transfer them to the hot grill and cook for 2 minutes on each side until browned.

5. Remove with a spatula, drizzle a little more honey on top of each, and eat while still hot.

MOZZARELLA, STRAWBERRY JAM, AND BASIL PANINI

Salty, sweet, and melted-cheesy, served on toast with fresh basil. You deserve better than Pop-Tarts, even if you are stoned.

1. Set a grill pan over medium heat.

2. Take 4 slices of bread and layer mozzarella cheese over them. Salt liberally, with more salt than you'd normally use. Trust me.

3. Cover the other 4 slices with the strawberry jam, and lay the basil slices on top.

4. Make sandwiches with one of each. Spray the pan with cooking spray and grill each side, pressing down with a panini press or a spatula for 2 to 3 minutes per side until the bread is golden brown and the cheese has melted.

8 slices thick country white bread

8 ounces fresh mozzarella cheese, sliced

Strawberry jam

16 fresh basil leaves

Kosher salt

Cooking spray

PEANUT BUTTER, CHOCOLATE, AND POTATO CHIP PANINI

Peanut butter. Chocolate. Potato chips. Bread. This is the most stoner-y stoner food ever. Goodbye, brain cells. My work here is done.

8 slices bread (any kind)

1 cup chocolate chips

One 9-ounce bag potato chips
   (Salty kettle chips work best.)

Peanut butter

Cooking spray

1. Set a grill pan over medium heat.

2. Take 4 slices of bread and spread ¼ cup chocolate chips on them.

3. Spread peanut butter on the other 4 slices. Break the potato chips up in the bag and crumble even amounts over the peanut butter slices.

4. Spray the pan with cooking spray.

5. Carefully assemble the sandwiches and gently press down with your hand to seal the deal.

6. Grill for 2 minutes on each side until golden brown and the chocolate has melted.

7. Mic drop. It's not getting better than this.

ACKNOWLEDGMENTS

A million thanks to: My editor, Michael Flamini, for cooking a crazy rice dish from a random recipe blog and contacting me, for taking a chance, believing in me, and making this whole thing happen. You changed my life. Lisa Pompilio, for a little bit of everything, especially the incredible cover. You rock harder than Slayer in 1986. April Rankin, for being my L.A. tour guide, and for the beautiful food styling and photography. You make me look good. Josh Lord, for the tattoo art, and Jonah Ellis for the hand-lettering on the cover. You guys are brilliant. (Lucky for me, I have some space left on my arm. . . .) My publisher, St. Martin's Press, for letting me be my ridiculous self. My agent, Brian DiFiore, for getting me paid for something I was already doing for free. Paul Synott, for the original logo. Without that logo, I probably wouldn't have bothered. Ronan Smyth, for supporting this project from even before the beginning. Next time I'm in Dublin, dinner and drinks are on me. Laura "Rebel Angel" Palmer, for giving me the idea for Vegetables Your Mom Ruined, and Chris Palmer, for always having my back. Dr. Mark Evces, for helping me set a goal and surpass it. The entire McNamara and Devash families, for all your love and support.

My parents, for your generosity, honesty, and for allowing me to take over your kitchen on 95-degree days in August to recipe-test Thanksgiving dinners—special thanks, Mom, for showing me how to stretch a buck when grocery shopping and, Dad, for trying quinoa. Shout out to Tom and Erika Devash, Shira and Peter Espinoza, and Yair Devash, for always sharing my recipes; it means a lot. My wife, the lovely and talented Meirav Devash, for being the taste-test victim for all the kitchen experiments that didn't make the blog or the book. Mary McNamara Barbuto, for being my favorite sister and my biggest supporter; Branden and the Barbuto clan (including Rosie, my newest taste-tester), for holding it down.

My Israeli mentors: Elka Devash, Eli Mordechai, Carmit Elkayam, and Eli Moradi, for influencing the way I cook. My grandmother (hell, everybody's grandmother), for the family style "Grandma cooking" that I view as the standard for excellence.

Chef Amanda Cohen, for taking meatless cooking to the next level, allowing me to intern, giving me a peek at what a wizard can do, and most of all, for being radder than Cru Jones. And my instructors and classmates at the Natural Gourmet Institute.

Vic Christopher, for being such a goddamn inspiration. Heather LaVine, Ricky and Christine Viola, for all the great meals. Grady Laird and Amy Keller Laird, for keeping the Kebapolis dream alive. Baz at Clash City Tattoo, for the killer logo tattoo, Brigette and Peter Smith, for all the Smithloft feedback (and chips). Team Burrows-Carpenter, Ilise Carter, Christine and Alex Colby, the Van Vrankens, the Florios, Josh Lewis, Alexis Colantonio, Robert Kennedy, Corrine Butler, Richard Callender, Melissa Bertoncini, Sarah Condry, the NakaBovens, the Robicellis, Paulie Gee, Eric Kun, Angel and Jeanette Colon, James Fitzsimmons, David Szucs, Angela Rivera, Liesa Goins and Doug Donaldson, Josh Nahas, Bianca Papas, the Borges family, Rich Luscombe, Kristin Perrotta, Rob Hart, Kristen Solury, Brenna Pack, Yelena Gitlin Nesbit, Brian Schenk, and Steve DeMartini, for believing and eating.

Leah Stewart, for copy editing. Vicki Lame, for graciously dealing with me and keeping things moving. Eric C. Meyer, for producing the thing. John Giuffo, for the kitchen throwdowns. Chris DiSanto, for helping me out when all I had was a funny name. And my writing teachers: Scott Cheshire, Hasanthika Sirisena, and Polly Kertis.

Dani from Sussex University, who saw me eating curry out of a tin as a teenager, and taught me how to cook so she'd never have to witness that again. I wish I could remember your last name. The men and women of the PAPD and the PBA. My South Brooklyn neighborhood family. My other crazy family, all you greasy fuckers in the NYC Rockabilly scene. A special thanks from Bobby Lupo to the Underground and Otherground. F the UG/OG. Everyone who ever read my Toss Your Own Salad Tumblr, cooked one of my recipes, e-mailed me, or shared a recipe with friends. You're all "a friend of ours."

INDEX